T0333629

HARNESS

A systemic approach: guaranteed to revolutionise your coaching

TESS COPE

HARNESS

First published in 2021 by

Panoma Press Ltd
48 St Vincent Drive, St Albans, Herts, AL1 5SJ, UK
info@panomapress.com
www.panomapress.com

Book layout by Neil Coe.

978-1-784529-62-8

The right of Tess Cope to be identified as the author of this work has been asserted in accordance with sections 77 and 78 of the Copyright, Designs and Patents Act 1988.

A CIP catalogue record for this book is available from the British Library.

This book is available online and in bookstores.

For those who have left us too soon

WHAT READERS ARE SAYING...

"Tess is a world class coach. The tools & practices she shares in this book demonstrate not just her technical knowledge and expertise, but her dedication to doing her own development work as a coach. This combination delivers exceptional value for clients and their organisations."

Tracey Gray, EVP: People, Ascential plc

"An inspiring and absorbing read that cuts through life's complex realities and provides a clear route to harnessing potential."

Mark Churchill, chief operating officer, Frontline Ltd

"An enjoyable read that is immediately relatable for busy executives. The toolkit is a notch sharper and goes deeper, to enable growth and change that lasts."

Jill Ford, head of HR, UK publishing at Bauer Media Group

"My experience of this approach to coaching with Tess is profound – I am able to harness the strength of my roots whilst being free to spread my wings. If more people could benefit from this approach, what an improvement in the quality of professional and private life we could all have!"

Aurelie Denayer, director of branding & communication, Proximus

"HARNESS, and the systemic perspective it passionately espouses, enables deep and meaningful conversations. Its tools will make you a better coach, and as a bonus, the reflective journey it invites you on may make you an even better person. All in all, a very valuable addition to your repertoire."

Narendra Laljani, management educator, strategy consultant, CEO coach

ACKNOWLEDGEMENTS

I've been continually crafting and honing my systemic approach over the last decade in a bid to ensure it adds significant value in and for organisations. As part of the learning journey, I believe we must also open ourselves up for doing our own 'inner work' as a rite of passage to offer it to others.

Before I acknowledge my teachers, I would like to bow to the founder of this approach, Bert Hellinger. Without his dedication and leadership, none of this would be possible.

Bert's work is renowned for identifying the governing principles of healthy systems, which we'll cover in chapter 2. His early work included the study of survivors of the Holocaust and his observations uncovered the phenomenon that unconscious patterns travel through the generations.

Hellinger's core methodology, constellations, was introduced in the mid 1990s. This approach is designed to illuminate and interrupt, where appropriate, the hidden dynamics and unconscious patterns within a human system.

Hellinger focused primarily on the family system. It was very quickly discovered that similar principles were true within the organisational realm. The methodology has been further developed and refined for the organisational context by a range of consultants, including Hunter Beaumont and Gunthard Weber.

Within this book, which is primarily aimed at coaching that takes place in the organisational context, we will refer to the constellation methodology in a number of ways, including 'systemic mapping', 3D mapping and creating 'living maps'.

I've had the privilege of learning with many systemic teachers over the course of the past decade. I'd like to particularly acknowledge those who have had a profound effect on me in the context of the whole person journey I embarked upon in 2011. In addition to facilitating my own growth and development, they have also enabled me to figure out how to integrate this approach so that it simultaneously adds real value for organisations and their leaders.

These teachers included but aren't limited to Judith Hemming (UK), Terry Wright (UK), Caroline Ward (UK), Jan Jacob Stam (The Netherlands) and Sarah Peyton (US).

How many times have you sat in front of a colleague or a 'client' and part way through the coaching conversation, you have the sensation that someone is holding up a mirror? You recognise their struggle and their challenges from your own experience. It is almost like you are simultaneously working with the younger, or perhaps current version, of yourself!

I am incredibly grateful to those clients who have been open and receptive to the incorporation of systemic coaching as a means of adding value to their development journey. Some of my most valuable learnings have taken place within the ongoing exploration, application and refinement process with them.

It is often said, that as coaches we find the clients (and team members) whose 'issues' align with our own areas of development. I welcome this. I believe it keeps us humble – it is a healthy reminder that none of us have got it all figured out. It keeps us at the right size and in the right place relative to those we are working with and the systems we each operate within.

And talking about wider systems, I also want to acknowledge the organisations I've been privileged to be part of, where the conditions that were created enabled this practice to be offered to, and developed with, the clients we served.

I experience the coaching process to be one that consistently provides a sense of mutual exchange. To all those people who have placed their trust in me, may I extend, a heartfelt 'thank you'.

The company we keep matters. I have often heard the phrase: "You are most heavily influenced by, and grow in line with, the five people you spend most of your time with."

In addition to continuous and intensive training, this approach requires extensive practice. I am privileged to have several peer groups as learning partners and, just like developing any other skill, there is no substitute for regular practice.

My systemic peer group has been gathering for the past six years with an overarching objective of honing our craft, developing new thinking and providing robust feedback to each other. I have grown and will continue to grow through this process. I'd like to extend a special thank you to a few core members of this group who have been by my side for most of the way, namely Emma Hackett and Alyse Ashton.

Finally, I'd also like to extend a huge thank you to my 'test readers' for their precious feedback as this book developed – your input has been invaluable. These include Emma Hackett, Alyse Ashton, Tracey Gray, Jill Ford, Alejandra Garcia, Mark Churchill, Aurelie Denayer, Jennifer Contreras, Narendra Laljani, and Yana Khaldi.

CONTENTS:

INTRODUCTION

Who is this book for?

This book is for you if you are ready to take your coaching skills to the next level. If you've found yourself trundling through the same repertoire of tried and tested coaching questions, it is probably time to freshen up your approach.

If you're frustrated by observing the people you are coaching remaining stuck in their repeating patterns, despite their sincere desire and ambition for a breakthrough, this book will provide you with new ways of approaching this dilemma.

You may be a leader where coaching is a critical aspect of your role or perhaps you are an external coach or consultant. In both cases, this is about levelling up and investing in your toolkit.

This systemic coaching approach is as relevant whether you are in an internal role or an external coach. As an external coach, I will often use the term 'client'. As a leader or an internal coach, the equivalent will be a team member or colleague for you.

Systemic coaching works with the whole person. As a philosophy, it acknowledges that what we have experienced outside of work influences who we are inside work and the other way around. It takes into consideration the systems that we have lived through and our heritage. It includes the whole spectrum of time – the past, present and the future.

In my view, it's time to acknowledge that sometimes we need to go back in order to move forward more quickly, more meaningfully and more sustainably. If you want to facilitate meaningful and sustainable transformation, coaching conversations need to go broader and deeper.

Getting optimum value from this book

Each chapter builds upon what has gone before. Regardless of the way in which you move through this book, I'd encourage you to pause in between chapters.

Take some time to fully digest and explore the methodology. Experiment with the recommended exercises for yourself. This book is intended to facilitate your own development as well as provide you with leading-edge coaching tools.

Create space for the insights that emerge, including those provoked by the 'percolations' that you'll find at the close of each chapter.

Chapters 1–5 outline the essential systemic principles, critical skills, and the classic systemic patterns you are likely to encounter within your leadership coaching.

Within chapters 6–12 you will find my 'HARNESS' coaching framework. Importantly, these chapters also include an overview of the interventions that are appropriate for each of the key systemic patterns that will be limiting potential.

Integrated throughout, you'll find real client examples of this approach. As you would expect, the client case studies have been anonymised to protect client confidentiality.

Before we begin...

A key principle of healthy systems is the element of inclusion, so it is only right that I start by acknowledging and including my own roots – these came first.

I was born and raised in Northern Ireland during 'The Troubles'. This was a time in my life when I had a vague sense of the complex and emotive layers just under the surface. Not all of these layers were immediately obvious, understood or wholly positive.

Northern Ireland is a small country of approximately 1.9 million, that experienced a sustained period of conflict. The concept of religion, and all that it represented, created deep unrest. There were countless traumatic events supposedly carried out in the name of opposing sides and belief systems. Over a period of 30 years, 3,500 fatalities were sustained.

As part of my survival strategy, I very quickly built the ability to look beyond the surface layer of people, places and conversations. In this context you needed to search for the undercurrent and gauge which 'side' you found yourself on, within any given moment. Things could shift quickly!

Whilst this backdrop meant that I witnessed and experienced significant trauma, I also gathered some essential life skills. I learnt how to live life in the moment, how to keep life's challenges in perspective and how to make the most of those precious moments in the warmth and comfort of your own tribe.

I may not have articulated it like this at the time, but I was learning how to navigate highly charged and complex environments and create safety in the process – skills that would stand me in good stead as I entered the complexity of organisational life and especially during times of change.

At my core, I am more resilient for having had these experiences and I absolutely know how to create safety for others.

Much later, in my professional career, I came across the systemic approach where one of the critical skills is to zoom back and look beyond the symptoms so that you can get to, and work with, the root cause. At a very deep level, this approach resonated with me and I have finally been able to fully integrate those essential life skills.

My experience is that the systemic approach enables profound transformation more quickly and more sustainably than most, if not all, of the coaching (and change) methodologies I have encountered in my 25 years of coaching within business.

Throughout this book, we'll dive into real examples that demonstrate the quantum shift that is possible with this approach, including but not limited to:

- Aruna, who transitioned from struggling to establish her place in her first senior leadership role to winning a global award for the turnaround of an underperforming division within 12 months.

- Derek, the CFO who moved from struggling to work with his CEO and not quite being part of the executive team to being seen and relied upon as a trusted colleague and taking up the role of sparring partner for the CEO. A transformation that ultimately enabled a seven-figure saving on the bottom line!

- Archie, who started from a very successful position but had hit a 'brick wall', to being freed up of the blind spots and limiting patterns that were rooted in his personal system. He moved through a series of successive promotions to acquire his ultimate role over the course of a few years.

- Kai, an incredibly ambitious and passionate specialist who had been appointed into his first managing director role of a European region that was underperforming. He initiated a series of robust and well-intentioned change initiatives only to find that the system went into gridlock. When the whole system, its history, and those that contributed to it, were acknowledged and taken into consideration, he was able to free up the system and bring the region back to its former glory.

- One of the world's leading publishers was challenged by a seismic shift in their market. By creating a multi-dimensional map of the changing landscape, they were able to identify the repositioning required and leverage a reshaped executive team to move the business towards a new vision and strategy.

I invite you to dive in now – create space to explore, experiment and take this opportunity to take your coaching expertise to the next level.

CHAPTER ONE

THE SYSTEMIC APPROACH

What do we mean by system?

When we use the term system, we are referring to a living entity within which humans interact. This can be a family system or an organisational system.

There are five defining characteristics of a system in this context.

1. Each system is part of a larger system

Some organisations are part of a larger group and no matter the size of an organisation, it is part of a sector and in a broader context, it is also part of society.

The characteristics of the larger system can often unconsciously cascade into the systems within. Furthermore, any unfinished business that has not been resolved in the larger system will show up in the smaller system. Just as unfinished issues in parents will show up in their children, so will be the case in organisations. A phrase that we often use in this context is: "As above, so below."

Unresolved issues in the larger system will show up in the
layers below

2. The survival mechanisms

There are three survival mechanisms in action within a system –
the personal, the collective (the system as a whole) and the force of
the upcoming future. The mechanisms on the personal dimension
are often conscious, whereas in the other two, the patterns are
often operating just outside of our awareness.

The fundamental need of the personal dimension is to establish
a sense of belonging. We will often make trade-offs, i.e. sacrifice
things that are important to us, in order to find a sense of belonging
within an organisation.

When we join a system, our fundamental need is to belong
– we will make personal sacrifices in order to fit in

The survival mechanism of the collective is to maintain or regain
its wholeness. It will often sacrifice individuals for the sake of
being complete. This is particularly evident when things that have
happened, or people who have influenced the organisation, are
excluded.

An example of this was a global FMCG organisation that was
struggling to hold on to talent in one of its regional leadership roles.
The pattern of a constant churn forced the wider organisation to
step back and get to the root cause.

The feedback from those who kept churning was that they couldn't
find their place and bring their best selves to the role or to the
business and so they moved on very quickly.

When the root cause was exposed, it became clear that a previous incumbent of the regional leadership role had been exited quickly without due care and consideration. The business did not acknowledge the difficulty or the inappropriate approach and tried to conveniently move on.

However, the history of what happened needed to be remembered, acknowledged and fully included before anyone could fully establish themselves in this regional leadership role. We call this phenomenon a 'burdened position'.

It is not possible to change what happened but we can ensure the narrative is accurate and therefore change the relationship with the history. Until such time as it is complete, the burden will continue. You can read more about this example in chapter 4.

The collective system is constantly seeking wholeness and will sacrifice the individual in this quest

---

The third survival mechanism is the evolutionary force of the upcoming future. Rather than us being in the driving seat as leaders of the system, this dimension is more about listening to what is needed. This is ultimately about ensuring that energy can flow, thereby enabling the system (and the people within it) to meet the highest potential.

This evolutionary force is often provoking us to consider what needs to come to an end in order that this potential can be realised. It may also be signaling that the organisation itself has, in fact, come to an end so that space for a new organisation can be created.

The upcoming future provokes us to consider what needs to come to an end, in order that energy can flow freely and potential can be realised

---

3. The overarching principles of a healthy system

ORDER:

- **History** that is fully acknowledged
- **A Sense of Place** – that enables each person to take their full responsibility and accountability
- **Mutual Exchange** – a balance of give and take
- **A Sense of Belonging**

ORIENTATION:

- **Clarity of Purpose** anchors and provides orientation
- **A clear flow of Leadership includes:** clarity, direction, clear decision making protocols, ways of working and reassurance during the uncertainty of emergent change

OPEN SYSTEM:

- An open system can **receive the impulses for change coming from the Emerging Future** – this is often asking us to consider 'WHAT NEEDS TO COME TO AN END?' (to make way for the new)

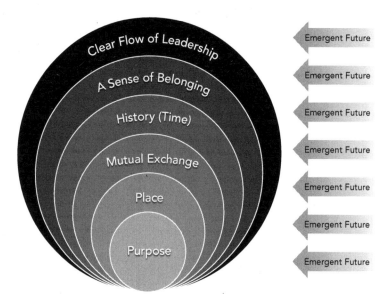

There are three fundamental principles that need to be taken care of in facilitating and sustaining a healthy system within which people thrive and can ultimately deliver their optimum performance. I often refer to these as 'The 3 x Os'.

Organisations need a level of:

Order

A sense of calm and order is facilitated when there is an acknowledgement of all that has happened and all those who have made significant contributions are included. When we know the history that lies behind us, it provides reassurance and solid grounding upon which people can stand.

When there is a solid ground of history behind us, and a sense of why we are here to orient us, then we can take our place within the system and understand how we can make our contribution. Taking our full place includes taking full responsibility and being held accountable for that contribution.

> Taking our full place includes taking full responsibility, being held accountable for that contribution – and feeling valued for it

There needs to be a sense of mutuality – a balance of give and take between the various parts of the system and between the organisation and the market it serves. This balance is not necessarily there in every transaction but is relevant when we look over time.

Within a family system, we have a secure and consistent sense of place. We will always be the first, second or third child – we understand where we fit, regardless of the unique makeup of the family. It is undeniable.

Within an organisational context, however, our sense of place is conditional upon making a consistent contribution to purpose. Mutuality in this context is feeling valued for that contribution.

Our place in an organisation is conditional upon making a consistent contribution to purpose

When each of these ordering principles is established, that fundamental survival mechanism of the individual, to belong, is made easier. This need to belong is as relevant to each employee as it is to one company that sits within a wider group of companies.

Orientation

A sense of orientation anchors the energy and provides direction and momentum. This includes the creation and clear communication of purpose, vision and being explicit about who the organisation is serving.

Purpose, vision and being clear about who the organisation is serving provides vital orientation

Openness

To progress and thrive, a system needs to remain open. Its boundaries need to be permeable enough to be able to notice the impulses for change coming from customers, the sector and the wider context. The system needs to have capacity to evolve and flow.

A system with solid boundaries that tries to maintain the status quo will shrivel and die in today's fast-moving society.

We'll cover examples of each of these principles in more detail within chapter 2.

> A system with solid boundaries that tries to maintain the status quo will shrivel and die in today's fast-moving society

4. The mindset required – problems are solutions

There is reframing of problems that is required with the systemic approach. Rather than being recruited into the mentality of solving issues, we are invited to pause and ask ourselves what the system is trying to communicate through this issue or repeating pattern.

We hold the belief that often the problems that are presented in the current context are merely solutions or a reaction to another part of the wider system.

Problems and especially if they are repeating, can be signals that some of the more fundamental principles have been disrupted.

> Repeating issues are often signals that some of the fundamental principles have been disrupted

Holding the widest possible context in mind, it can be helpful to pause, zoom back and ask ourselves a few questions, such as:

- How long has this issue been happening?
- What is the system trying to communicate through this issue/problem or repeating pattern?
- What could be the very good reason for this?
- What is the unmet need of the wider system?
- What is it trying to move towards?

By acknowledging that problems might be a solution for something much more fundamental, we are more likely to identify the root cause and ultimately enable a healthy flow to return.

5. The methodology

This approach is ultimately aiming to facilitate two key movements:

- Surface and release the limiting patterns
- Free up the system to move towards its highest potential

The methodology has been designed to uncover and magnify the dynamics and patterns that are active, particularly those at the unconscious level. This process brings to the surface that which is happening just outside of our awareness.

The systemic approach requires you to go beyond the logical and analytical, and to work at the opposite end of the spectrum, i.e. to work with what is not necessarily seen or tangible in the first instance. This is called the phenomenological approach. It is about working with the felt sense, the visceral experience and your intuition as it emerges.

It asks us to hold the premise that what we experience on a visceral level can be viewed as potential data that may be symptomatic of what is actually going on for the individual, in the organisation, or the wider ecosystem.

We facilitate clarity, perspective and provide a navigation path through the complexities of the whole system via a mapping process.

Once the system is mapped, we are looking for the areas that have become entangled, stuck or toxic, and keep unpacking the layers until we get to the root cause.

It's about getting a sense of the patterns, those that repeat, and getting to the source of these patterns. To do that, you need to cultivate a special attitude of seeing. Instead of zooming in, you need to zoom out to see the system as a whole, and even as part of the larger system it belongs to.

By appropriately adjusting the map and introducing the appropriate interventions, we can deal with the root causes and release the entanglements that will enable the system, and those within it, to settle. This combination of precise and spacious steps enables the movements mentioned above.

What does the system need from leadership?

As you would expect, leadership is critical. However, rather than consider what leaders want from the system (and those within it) it can be helpful to shift the focus to what the system needs from leaders.

Shift your perspective:
What does the system need from leaders?

Put simply, systemic leadership is about acknowledging that all that went before contributed to what is possible today. It's about ensuring individuals can find and take their place quickly, creating an environment whereby all parts of the system can perform at their best, providing an aligned sense of direction and designing the organisation in the context of its ecosystem, so that it can constantly evolve.

Context is everything

As a coach, it is critical to acknowledge the reality that the people we are working with find themselves in. Great coaching cannot happen in a vacuum.

The reality is that there is always going to be a myriad of disrupting forces in the ecosystem at any one point in time. As we came out of the pandemic of 2019–2021, one of the challenges for organisations was the strategic need to develop talent and equip people with new skills.

The backdrop however, based on a recent study by Monster[1], is that almost 70% of employees are showing signals of exhaustion and burnout due to the extended period of remote working. It has been a period where the boundaries between 'work' and 'home' have become well and truly blurred.

The irony is that organisations have, in a lot of cases, experienced improvements in productivity, but if we consider some of the most fundamental needs of human beings, such as a sense of belonging and connection, this productivity is not sustainable if people are working in constant isolation.

In today's society, talking about mental health is becoming more normal which is just as well, when we take into consideration that, according to Mind, one of the primary mental health charities based in the UK, one in four people will experience a mental health problem of some kind.

Add to this, most organisations are radically rethinking their working environment. It's a complex mix of influencing factors that include, but is not limited to, strategic direction, geographic footprint, the scale of the business, the location of the headquarters, the nature of the work involved and the desired culture of the organisation.

Some organisations have transmitted clear directives around being office-based, others are at the other end of the continuum and letting employees decide for themselves. And of course, there are some taking the middle ground and recommending a balance of both.

There is no perfect model, but within our coaching conversations, it's vital to bear in mind that one of the most fundamental needs for individuals to bring their best selves is that unconscious but profound need to belong.

Our role

As I mentioned earlier, our role is to facilitate movement. Ultimately, we are in service to enable two key movements with this work.

1. Release any limiting patterns that might be hindering flow, freedom and performance.

2. Create a sense of clarity of the upcoming future so that individuals, groups and/or organisations can move towards their destiny.

The task is to free up the areas that have become entangled, stuck or toxic, to enable movement

Critical competencies

There are four critical competencies to master when working systemically.

Zoom back and wide

One of the critical competencies is about pausing before you react. It's about learning how to zoom back and wide, to look beyond the obvious, to stay curious and get to the source of issues.

This is as relevant for employee anxieties, concerns and wellbeing as it is about organisational vitality and performance. There are often strong links between what is happening at the individual dimension and what is playing out within the organisational context. Don't assume these are always separate events.

By delaying, or worse still, ignoring these difficult conversations and issues, the consequences on performance, potential and bottom-line performance might only get worse.

I believe this is an opportunity to broaden and deepen the coaching conversation. The systemic approach invites you to consider the individual as a whole person. This involves looking beyond the surface, getting to the root cause and going further and deeper than perhaps you may have done before.

Be comfortable with not knowing

This is about building your skill and comfort in working with the uncomfortable, the complex and the messy reality that your client/colleague finds themselves in.

You need to be comfortable with not knowing, and willing to stay curious; pay attention to what you notice in yourself as you listen and observe.

Listening to the system

You need to listen to what you notice beyond the cognitive, practical and logical. You need to be able to listen to your own embodied sense of what you are picking up and to be able to stay in the not knowing for longer than perhaps you would normally feel comfortable.

By really listening and observing what we sense, we open up another channel for understanding what is really going on. The phenomenological approach means that we also include our embodied experience of the situation, no matter how subtle.

When we are listening in this way, it can be helpful to sense check which system is communicating through this individual. It might be that their personal system is playing out in the organisation setting.

I often find that someone's dominant leadership style and their reactions to situations are heavily influenced by their personal system without them realising it. The nature of the coaching in that situation is about helping them to separate out these two contexts, so that some conscious choices can be made.

Listen out for which system the client is speaking from

It might also be the case that the scenario is wholly driven by organisational dynamics in the system but these can still trigger our personal hot buttons, especially if there are unresolved personal issues sitting in the background.

There is often a complex web of systems in action, and part of our role as coach is to help our client also zoom back so that they can see the various layers for what they are.

When we are an internal resource, we have special access to those deeper layers of the system. When we develop our phenomenological approach, it enables us to make sense of what we are intuitively picking up and helps us to navigate between being on the dance floor alongside our colleagues and zooming back to view things from the balcony.

In summary, there's a different quality and depth of listening required for this work. You need to be able to listen to how the system is communicating through the individual, in their language, and in their embodied sense of what's going on. You are listening in order to understand the whole and their place in the whole.

Our first priority in listening is not to fix, but to understand

We are searching for the root cause and to unleash what wants to flow

---

Precision questioning

The final competency that needs to be developed is the precision of your questioning.

When we are listening to the system, our questions are aimed at surfacing the tension, unpacking the patterns, and getting to the root cause. This does not always entail moving in a straight line – we often need detours.

Whilst our questions need to be precise, they also need to create spaciousness – if they are too tight or too fast, the system will close down rather than open up.

Our questions need to be precise AND create spaciousness

You will discover a portfolio of questions to add to your systemic toolkit throughout this book.

Create a safe container

The degree of movement that is possible will be influenced by the level of safety mindfully created by the coach and the degree of safety actually felt by the individual or group. These can be different things, especially if the coach is moving too fast. Within the systemic approach, we often use the phrase: "Go slow in order to go fast later."

If you pick up resistance at this early stage, something needs attention. Engage in this conversation early. This is as true in the individual coaching context as it is in a group coaching or group facilitation context.

Go slow in order to go fast later

The coach needs to be hyper-vigilant of what the client is ready for and what they may be wary about. This is not always obvious. Vulnerability needs careful handling. If you start unpacking the layers too quickly or too directly, they may start withdrawing – it is important to work at the pace they are truly ready for.

This potential level of fragility or vulnerability is further complicated when the context significantly changes during times of crisis. The perceptions of strength and weakness in someone's leadership may flip.

Individuals who are used to being structured and in control may have been perceived as the strongest members of a team. When they are in the midst of chaos that is outside of their control, they may suddenly feel very exposed.

By contrast, those who would normally be more spontaneous and prefer to go with the flow may have previously been perceived as flimsy or less reliable. They may shift to be the ones who are seen as more robust, as they can rely on their innate agility and ability to flex and flow moment by moment.

A classic case of this is through the period of the Covid crisis in 2020–2021, when almost every norm in terms of ways of working had to be reimagined on a scale that would have previously been hard to contemplate. Those strong, assertive leaders who were accustomed to being in control and scoping out the strategic direction, were potentially the ones feeling most vulnerable and in need of support.

Providing this support in a collective context needs subtle care so that the vulnerable do not feel exposed. They need to feel implicitly understood and in a 'container' that can hold the group as they navigate through the process.

> You need to create a 'container' that enables the most fragile and vulnerable to stay involved in the process

When you are coaching inside the system, it is critically important that you are clear on boundaries and, in particular, how the information that is disclosed in the confidential space of a coaching session will be utilised, if at all.

> Being clear on the rules of engagement around confidentiality is critical

Being clear on the rules of engagement around confidentiality is critical. These will be slightly different depending on your role. If your role is as an internal coach in a large organisation, you may wish to contract with the individual differently than perhaps the boundaries that might be established within a line manager and direct report relationship.

This confidentiality piece needs to be taken care of from the outset of the coaching relationship so that you can create a safe space and enable appropriate and meaningful disclosure.

The environment matters

In addition to considering the right timing and pacing, it is also vital to be aware of the optimum environment for coaching.

Today's office environment is often open-plan. Where you do have some separation of space, it is often created by glass – a space I fondly call the 'goldfish bowl'.

Whilst any separate space can be helpful, assuming it is soundproof of course, it doesn't always create the safe container that is required when you need to start the mapping process mentioned earlier and start unpacking the layers, i.e. take the conversation deeper.

By changing the environment, you can help prepare the individual for a shift in the quality and depth of the coaching conversation

Take people away from their standard environment, get them away from their desk. If you are connecting virtually, encourage them to sit somewhere else for these kinds of conversations – the environment really makes a difference.

The place of the coach

The coach has a pivotal role. It is an opportunity to help them navigate this reality, to find a path through it so that they can drive the results the business requires, whilst finding a way to realise their highest potential.

When I am working with a coaching client, I'm always asking myself two fundamental questions: What is my role? What is my place?

One of the classic foundations of coaching is to be aware when you unconsciously shift into mentoring mode. It is important to discern what is needed and be careful not to move to a place where you feel bigger or better than them.

The coach is at their most powerful and valuable when operating from a place of service. A helpful belief for the coach to hold is that the client already has everything they need – even if they aren't yet aware of it, or perhaps don't yet understand how to utilise it.

The most enabling place for the coach is alongside the client

---

The role of the coach is to light the path forward, one step at a time. This probably sounds so obvious but common sense does not always prevail.

It is so easy for the coach to be triggered into their own ego, to race ahead, to make assumptions and lean too heavily on their own experience and inappropriately project this onto the individual.

This projection or inappropriate pace will only serve to trigger the individual to unconsciously pull back – either immediately because they sense the coach has 'taken over', or when they realise further down the line that a relationship of dependency has been created between coach and client.

Being the right size and in the right place, relative to the client, was one of my biggest learnings in my systemic coaching training and from that learning, this poem emerged.

I'M HERE, ON YOUR LEFT

I'm here on your left

I'm not too big and,

I won't make you small

I'm here on your left

So you can stand tall.

I'm here on your left

To be your Thought Partner,

In whatever form you need

I'm here on your left

So you can take the lead.

I'm here on your left

To provide the stimulus,

And hold the space

I'm here on your left

So you can make your decisions

With due consideration and grace.

Summary

We've covered a lot in this first chapter. Here are some of the headlines…

There are five defining characteristics of a system:

- Every system is part of a larger ecosystem.

- There are three survival mechanisms (individual, collective and the upcoming future).

- There are three principles that enable a healthy system. These include a sense of order, robust orientation and a system that is open to receive the impulses of the evolving future.

- A mindset shift is required. Repeating problems are often solutions from another dimension of the system.

- The methodology asks us to go beyond the logical and analytical. The phenomenological approach includes our embodied experience.

The overall ambition is to facilitate two key movements:

1. Release any limiting patterns that might be hindering flow, freedom and performance.

2. Create a sense of clarity of the future so that forward momentum can be initiated and sustained.

Creating safety is an essential ingredient – without it, we cannot access the deeper layers. These include dynamics within the personal realm, the organisational system and the patterns and dynamics that belong to each.

Before moving forward, sufficient attention and respect must be given to the history and heritage. When this is given its rightful place and the critical competencies are deployed, the movement can be fast and sustainable.

The critical competencies include being able to zoom back and wide, being comfortable with not knowing, listening at another level and deploying questions that can be deployed with equal degrees of precision and spaciousness.

This speed of movement is predicated on the degree to which you built a safe container. Be conscious of the environment where you open things up and ensure to operate at a pace your client is ready for and to a depth you feel equipped to handle.

It's helpful to turn the question of leadership 'on it's head' and ask "what does the system need from leaders?" rather than the other way around.

The most effective place of the coach is alongside the client – be careful not to become too big and create dependency. This will ultimately weaken the client and the system.

Finally, ensure you stay in the place of enabling and being of service. A helpful phrase I have picked up recently may help you to remain mindful of this:

'Don't be a sage on the stage – be a guide on the side'

CHAPTER TWO

SYMPTOMS OF AN UNHEALTHY SYSTEM

Exceptional performance and realisation of potential is reliant upon the right environment – the ecosystem matters.

When there is a distortion around the history or disruption in the fundamental principles of order, orientation and openness outlined in chapter 1, limiting patterns will emerge. These patterns will repeat and may impact at the individual or collective level. They ultimately erode performance and limit the degree to which potential can be realised.

These fundamental principles are like invisible but powerful forces in a system. They have a profound impact on the ability of the organisation to flow and evolve towards its future. They are not necessarily immediately visible or tangible but will stealthily penetrate every aspect of how daily work is experienced by those in the system.

It is often the visceral experience of a lack of energy, vitality and flow, together with a sense of unspoken friction, heaviness or stuckness that makes these principles more obvious.

By understanding these principles and how they show up in the system, they provide us with a way of decoding what we are intuitively picking up. They are relevant whether you are working with the whole system, a team, a function or an individual.

The fundamental principles provide us with a way of decoding what we are intuitively picking up

---

What to look out for

The most prevalent symptoms of an unhealthy system include:

1. Rigidity of the organisation (or key leaders). This can manifest as a lack of ability to flex or move, especially during times of change.

2. The organisation (or a part of it) appears to be 'standing still' or 'frozen' in time.

3. A significant part of, or a group within, the organisation is primarily focused on the past, and often with a sense of nostalgia.

4. Broken connections – there is a split in the workforce.

5. Lack of flow between functions or between 'head office' and the regions/divisions.

6. Repeating reports of tension and friction that have no rational explanation despite changes in leadership.

7. Loss or outsourcing of a critical capability.

8. Key positions have a constant churn regardless of the quality of talent that is recruited into these roles.

Client example

"Our financial performance is poor and we're losing our best people to our competitors, despite having the best product and being well respected in the market – it just doesn't make sense. What is going on?", was the frustration, shared by John.

John was a newly appointed CEO of a privately owned, London-based organisation. The company had been established a few decades earlier but had not been profitable for some time. It was inefficient in terms of its processes and was losing some of its best people to the competitors despite having a great reputation for its products.

He wanted to understand the size of the challenge he had in front of him as quickly as possible. He grasped the opportunity to zoom back and engaged the whole organisation in a review of the health of the system. A wealth of quantitative and qualitative data was facilitated through a cultural diagnostic tool, that also helped to surface insights on the ordering forces mentioned above.

He discovered that the system was organised more like a university, where intellectual horsepower was valued more highly than revenue or profit. In terms of leading principles, product quality and precision came before customers.

The sense of purpose seemed to be about creating perfection of the product in of itself rather than the delivery of the product into the market. Employees who were close to the product were highly regarded and those further away from this intellectual production process felt undervalued.

The commercial dimension of the enterprise was not on the radar for employees and the level of energy and vitality was low. There was an alarmingly high rate of 30% toxicity (i.e. of all the activity in the organisation, 30% of it was stuck, duplicated or frustrated energy).

Of paramount importance when working systemically, is the ability to stay free of judgment. The first task is to surface what is, and acknowledge there will be, or will have been, a very good reason why this is so. From this platform, you can discern the appetite and readiness for movement and determine what is the best next step.

He discovered very little urge or impetus for evolution in terms of how they organised themselves or how they met the needs of their customers. In short, if John was going to transform the leading principles whereby the commercials were at least as important as the quality of the product, there was a lot of work to do!

His action plan covered some of the fundamentals such as putting the customer at the heart of the business, addressing supply chain issues that would ensure the product reached its destination on time.

John was determined to bring the vitality back by ensuring everyone had a voice, a sense of place and clarity on how they could contribute to a new sense of purpose. The blockages and disruptions in those ordering forces were surfaced and over a period of 18 months, a comprehensive action plan was co-created and implemented with the management community.

It took a lot of heavy lifting and a new executive team at the helm but two years later, this organisation was almost unrecognisable.

There was clarity and alignment around purpose, employees felt more empowered, there was more clarity on how decisions were made and alignment on the core values was achieved; people could find their right place and felt valued for their contribution regardless of where they were in the organisation.

There was a healthy level of mutual exchange between employer and employee and between the organisation and its customers. Vitality was emerging and from a commercial standpoint, double digit growth (revenue and profit) had returned. Sales were on an upward trajectory and staff turnover was reduced by 30%.

The diagnostic was repeated and the level of toxicity had been reduced from 30% to 13%. There was still some work to do to get below the recognised healthy level of 10% or less, but this was seen as being within reach.

Start with the history

From a systemic perspective, time has three dimensions – history, the current reality and the future. The dimensions that often need most attention are history and the present. When these are in good shape, and the fundamental principle of an open system is in focus, the future can evolve.

Is it truthful and complete?

What has happened before needs to be complete, included and acknowledged. This inclusion allows employees to feel rooted, to fully leverage the experience and expertise gathered to date and to be fully present with what is here now.

When we exclude aspects of our history, part of us is still metaphorically left behind and held hostage by what has gone before – ultimately, this restricts what is possible today.

Client example

As you may have read within my introduction, a big part of my personal history was growing up in Northern Ireland during 'The Troubles'. As a family, we witnessed and were directly impacted by many traumatic events. For a large part of my life, and as a way of surviving, I chose to leave the country, to exclude these events from my consciousness with an intention to get on with life.

On one level, by excluding this, I could keep my focus on building a new life, working hard and looking forward. On a more fundamental and deeper level, however, the consequence of this approach was that some of my energy was locked down. Part of me remained rooted in the trauma of the past. Ultimately, I wasn't fully available to step into my highest potential because part of me was left behind.

Through my systemic training, I was ready to lean in and do some of my own inner work. I acknowledged and included this experience as part of my history. I took time to appreciate how what had happened made some sense, when the context of the wider ecosystem of Northern Ireland and the thirty-year battle that was coming to a tipping point at the time, was taken into consideration even if I didn't agree with some of the specific events.

Importantly, I also acknowledged the gifts I gained from this experience and by doing so, I was able to fully honour my history, leverage these gifts and move forward in the world. You can hear more about this story, when I spoke about it in public for the first time, in my SpeakUpChallenge here: https://vimeo.com/346399906

When you can give what has happened (and those who have contributed to it) its right place in history, then everything can settle. It enables you to be fully present in the here and now, and truly engage with what is calling you – including your future potential.

This is as true at the individual level as it is for the organisation. When we try to exclude significant aspects of our history, the individual (or organisation) is weakened.

Turning away, moving on and 'pretending' it didn't happen doesn't work – it's not that simple. When we try to avoid something, we are unconsciously excluding it.

One of the phrases that is often utilised in this work is: "You become what you try to avoid." If we try to exclude something or someone from our history or a part of ourselves, we will inadvertently become that at some unconscious level because the system is constantly seeking wholeness.

You become what you try to avoid

You might recognise this phenomenon within family systems, in particular. It is not unusual for a child to vow that they never want to be like their parent and actively try to avoid this, only to find that later in life, those same attributes show up in abundance!

The system is constantly seeking wholeness – when we exclude key elements, the system will find a way to bring them back

---

From a systemic point of view, excluding something means that it just ends up coming back into the system in another way, through another avenue, through another person, through another role, until such time as it is fully remembered and able to take its rightful place in the system.

Within a coaching context, it is not unusual to hear individuals narrate difficult experiences and share how they just decided to move on. And yet, these experiences are often the richest origin of their most valuable resources and have often triggered the birth of their core values.

Take some time to clarify and harvest these resources so that they can be consolidated and built upon.

Client Example

"We have done all the analysis, the recovery plan is in place, everyone has been involved, we have the right people on the right things — but nothing is moving — what is going on?", said Kai as he buried his head in his hands.

Kai was a passionate, ambitious and well-established senior leader. He had been moving through the ranks of the global business for the past five years and as part of his career progression, he was promoted into his first managing director role, heading up one of the European regions in a global FMCG business.

His predecessor had been in place for a considerable period, as had the senior leadership team, which he inherited. They really understood the business and quite a few of them had 'grown up' through the ranks of the organisation. There was a wealth of knowledge and experience in this team.

The region had previously been one of the highest performing regions in Europe, however there had been a level of steady decline over the last few years. This was particularly evident on the major product categories. Kai's brief was to address the performance issue.

As all new senior leaders aspire to do, he wanted to make his mark as part of his ongoing career trajectory. After a period of thorough analysis, he charted a course of high-impact activity to transform the business.

However, within this drive, there was a lack of acknowledgement of the contributions from his predecessor, the cultural norms of the country, and the significant efforts of those who had been in the team for a while. In fact, at times the opposite was true whereby there was a negative critique on how the business had been led and managed in the preceding years.

A range of simultaneous projects was launched – each designed to transform a critical aspect of the business on a scale that would mean, when complete, the business would be almost unrecognisable. Each workstream was built upon rigorous commercial analysis and teams of highly intelligent people were rallied around the plan. No expense was spared in this transformation plan.

Instead of driving sales, the reality was that the business became paralysed. On face value, everything that was initiated made complete sense, the right people were assigned to the most appropriate projects and it seemed that there was energy for the change, but the reality was that the business went into gridlock.

When he zoomed back and peeled back the layers in an effort to get to the root cause of the paralysis, it became very obvious that the lack of appreciation of who and what was before, triggered an unconscious resistance to this ambitious plan.

Individuals were not consciously or explicitly rebelling but at some level there was a lack of engagement and energy for what needed to be done. This was most evident within the operational aspects of the business.

There were continuous challenges in the fundamentals of getting product through the supply chain and into the market – this area of the business was previously 'running like clockwork' and without too much effort. It just didn't make any sense.

The intervention that enabled a shift involved acknowledging and honouring the history of the region. This included acknowledging the previous leader and their efforts, even if some of those activities didn't make sense at some level. Those experiences had provided insights and learnings for all who came later. The decades of previous successes and all those that contributed to it were explicitly acknowledged and celebrated.

When it was made clear that the next phase was only possible because of all that had happened before, and all those who contributed to it, things started to settle.

Over a period of a few months, the recurring supply chain issues were freed up, energy and vitality returned, the resistance that could be sensed previously relaxed and the results followed. Sales growth and profitability flowed and the desired transformation got underway.

Is there an avoidance of the difficulties and pain points?

This aspect can easily be overlooked. The intention within this domain is to ensure that all that has happened before, and that which is active in the current reality, is fully acknowledged. This includes the pain, the difficult events and anything that has been excluded or avoided up until now, together with the consequences.

The truth needs to be acknowledged without judgement – keep it to the facts of what has happened, the consequences and where they have been experienced.

Ensure enough time and space is spent in this phase – it is tempting to sweep over it, in a bid to move on. This phase can amplify and stimulate the impetus for movement.

There is immense power in acknowledging the truth of what is

Can the system move?

From a systemic perspective, the future has two dimensions:

- The Planned Future, that which we want to make happen. This is where we set our intentions, create our strategies and to some extent, operate from an ego state and belief that we are in control. Within this context, the question we are asking ourselves is: What do I want to do with my life?

- The Upcoming or Evolutionary force of the Future, that is coming towards us, and to a great extent, is outside of our control. In this context, the question here would be more like: What does life want from me (or us)?

When working with the upcoming future, your role as a coach is to help the individual engage with this evolutionary force, and find a way to move in flow with it, whilst remembering that this dimension of the future is often asking them to consider what do they need to stop doing in order to create space for the new.

It is about suspending, or perhaps even deleting, the should-dos. These are most likely coming from either their ego, their predecessor, their boss or someone else from the systems they belong to. The weight of these expectations can leave individuals feeling constrained, closed down and directed rather than agile, open to what is possible and evolving.

It is about helping them get a sense of their highest potential and to align with this flow, such that they can move with it rather than it feel like continuous heavy lifting.

Here are a few questions that can be helpful for the client to hold, when connecting with this evolutionary force:

1. What do I need to put down/stop in order to free myself up to what wants to come?

2. If I listen to my inner knowing, what is calling me forward?

3. What does my gut instinct (intuition) already know about this best next step?

Client Example

"If only I knew which of these options was the right one for me, right now", was Laura's plea.

Laura had established herself as a key member of the leadership team. She had built her credibility and gravitas over the course of this current assignment but this was soon going to be coming to an end.

She needed to find the right opportunity that would ensure she continued to develop and progress – an essential element for her in her professional context but this also had to be balanced with being the main 'income generator' for her family.

From a variety of sources, including directly connecting with her stakeholders near and far, she was aware of a variety of forthcoming opportunities in the wider global organisation, one of which included relocating her family to another continent.

A session was dedicated to really tuning into her gut instinct around each of those options and gathering some insights on her optimum next step. She needed to ensure she balanced the right choice for her career and the needs of her family.

We utilised the process that engages the evolutionary force of the emerging future outlined in detail within chapter 10. Laura mapped out her options and took time to sense check which of them felt most congruent for her. This process enables additional and important information to be surfaced more explicitly and subsequently explored, as required.

She identified a low level of anxiety with one of the options and was encouraged to stay curious about it, rather than dismiss it immediately.

Her confidence in her own intuition meant that she was able to sense check this phenomenon and get underneath that sense of anxiety so as to understand where it might have been coming from. This additional step helped her to determine if this was a serious roadblock or merely an obstacle that could be dealt with.

Having worked her way through each of those options and trusting that gut instinct, she was able to get down to a shortlist of two roles.

This deeper intelligence gathering enabled Laura to be reassured that she was asking the right questions, with the right stakeholders, around this shortlist of two opportunities within the business, before making her final choice and relocating her family.

Is there a balance of giving and taking?

Healthy, sustainable relationships need a balance of giving and taking over time

This is as true between individuals as it is between organisations and their employees and finally between organisations, their customers and society as a whole.

We can relate to this principle in our own relationships – think about a relationship when you have realised you have been overgiving. This can only be sustained for so long. At some point, you will pull back or indeed the 'debt' becomes too heavy for the other person and so they would rather pull away from the relationship than keep receiving.

This is as true in our personal relationships as it is in commercial relationships. Think about the principle of giving a generous tip in a restaurant or a hotel – you automatically trigger the sensation in the recipient of more giving. At an unconscious level, they feel called upon to even things up and so they enact this by giving something more or going out of their way to look after you, in return.

When exchange is not equitable, the system will keep surfacing the issue in an effort to bring attention to it so that things can be balanced out. This is not always experienced as a positive reminder!

There will be times when mutuality is not possible, for example when a business is being restructured and people who have dedicated extensive years of service, are losing their jobs despite a significant contribution to the organisation. In these instances, it is key that they are recompensed appropriately, and if that's not possible, then the imbalance in exchange needs to be explicitly acknowledged.

How commercial companies handle the recall of deficient products highlights this principle really well. Recent research shows that 87% of consumers would trust brands and remain loyal if organisations handle product recalls honourably, honestly and responsibly.

A poor example of this can be evidenced in the recent scandal of VW Audi in 2015 around the cover up of emission rates. VW Audi was found to be covering up a software error which alleged their cars were recording emission rates of up to 40 times worse than those recorded under laboratory conditions. Upon discovery of the scandal, the appropriate cars were recalled, however, at a cost to their reputation.

Can everyone find their place?

Within our families, we have a clear sense of place. We are and will always be the first, second or third child in the sequence and even when we are part of a blended family, this certainty of place is more absolute than it might be within the organisational context.

Within an organisation, things are more complex. Our sense of place is conditional on consistent performance and providing a contribution to the organisation's purpose. This is reliant upon clarity of the purpose and a robust cascade into each of the functions and teams so that everyone understands where their area fits into the overall plan.

Employees need a place from which they can make their contribution to the purpose of the organisation and feel valued for that contribution

---

When there is a lack of clarity of the purpose, individuals (and functions) can be pulled out of their 'right place'. They can become too big or too small, and in both cases, this will create an unhelpful dynamic in the system.

Client example

"Is she up to this? Have we made the wrong recruitment decision?", was the noise in the system about Aruna.

Aruna was promoted to head up the highest revenue-generating division of the business with which came a seat in the leadership team. This division was responsible for over 30% of the overall revenue but had been experiencing a decline over the previous 18 months.

The key theme coming out of Aruna's 360-stakeholder feedback from her peers was that she wasn't fully taking her place 'at the table'.

At a behavioural level, this showed up as holding back, not contributing to the conversation and behind the scenes, there were lots of questions. She was questioning herself on everything and asking her peers for their advice. This wasn't just happening in her work context.

On the surface, it was seen as a confidence issue. As a result, her peers were questioning her ability to steer their most important division out of a turndown and her colleagues were stepping into the void. For Aruna's team, it was very unclear who they should refer to for decisions which was creating more confusion and delays in the schedule of the turnaround plans.

It was fair to say that the decision to promote her was being questioned in some parts of the team.

Our work within the coaching context was to get to the root cause of this issue on place – when we peeled back the layers, this was not as simple as a confidence issue. We'll come back to Aruna's story in the next chapter.

Who belongs?

A sense of belonging is the final and potentially the most crucial of the ordering principles of a healthy system and as described in chapter 1, is one of the underpinning survival mechanisms.

During times of significant disruption, when the architecture of the system is being reimagined, this is often the only fundamental principle that you can rely upon.

People will withstand unimaginable disruption when they feel that they belong. A strong sense of belonging enables employees to stay with the organisation and remain standing 'shoulder to shoulder' whilst everything else is being dismantled in preparation of what needs to happen next.

Their loyalty to each other can withstand a lack of clarity in most other areas. This only serves to underline its importance within the organisational context.

The sense of belonging provides essential glue in times of crisis

---

Creating and sustaining a sense of belonging needs to be ever present on the agenda of leadership. It is the element that needs most attention by leaders during times of crisis.

One of the prerequisites for a sense of belonging is the attribute of inclusiveness – an essential ingredient of leadership.

What's the point?

For a healthy system, and truly engaged employees, it is essential for employees to have clarity on the purpose of the organisation so that they can find their place in terms of how they can meaningfully contribute towards it. The systemic function of purpose is to provide orientation and an anchor point for everyone to gravitate towards.

Purpose provides vital orientation

It is important to highlight that purpose is not exclusively an inside job. Whilst it is essential to ensure resources, talents, expertise and experience are fully leveraged, it's also helpful to acknowledge who/what the organisation serves.

From a systemic perspective, purpose is about being clear on what the company exists for and the problems it solves for society and its customers.

Being purposeful and operating as a responsible business is rising in importance in today's more informed society. This necessitates the inclusion of multiple stakeholders in the value chain, thinking beyond short-term results and driving a multidimensional bottom line, i.e. looking more holistically and incorporating metrics beyond profit and shareholder value. Latest research on companies that have got this balance right are showing that they are outperforming others by a factor of 30%.

It is no longer good enough to espouse driving shareholder value and driving performance results as the reason for being. People are waking up to and becoming more passionate about a more holistic approach to doing business. With this backdrop in mind, it is becoming ever more crucial that this clarity around purpose is cascaded through the ecosystem and evidenced in more organisations waking up to the concept of a triple bottom line[2].

When done well, purpose informs the strategy, culture and core values of an organisation. Because purpose is about being of service, it evolves over time. This may be in response to evolving customer/client/beneficiary needs and the evolutionary force of the upcoming future.

When working with leaders in a coaching context, it is not unusual to be helping them uncover and articulate purpose on a minimum of two dimensions. Firstly, as an individual leader and secondly, with regard to the purpose for their area of the business.

It is strongly recommended that you put priority on the individual aspect of purpose first. Purposeful businesses need purposeful leaders at the helm.

When individuals have a clear sense of purpose of their own, this enables them to feel rooted and anchored in something bigger than themselves. Purpose enables individuals to give a very clear yes or a very clear no to the multitude of tasks that are continuously added to the to-do list.

Without the anchoring effect of purpose, chaos can ensue and if it is happening at the top of the organisation, you can be ensured it will be happening elsewhere. One of my favourite and most helpful systemic phrases to keep in mind in this context is:

'As above, so below'

Client Example

"I'm a bit overwhelmed — everything is up in the air — I'm not sure what to do first."

James was a specialist who found himself in a role that was being made redundant as a consequence of a significant restructure. Having lived through the difficult challenge of making his old team redundant, he was tasked with setting up a brand-new global function, designed to drive the growth agenda in collaboration with the various regions of a global business.

He was making that classic transition from a role where he had deep expertise and a lot of control, into a role that required new skills and was part of a matrix setup. It was all about making things happen through influence with limited autonomy. This was new territory for James on many dimensions.

One of the early areas of focus within the coaching journey was to focus on the two dimensions of purpose namely, find/rediscover his own sense of purpose and figure out what the new global function was there to do and how it fitted into the wider ecosystem.

It would have been very easy to get drawn into working on the purpose of the new function first and then retrofit his own sense of purpose into this.

However, the danger of being pulled into the purpose for the new function first, would mean that James would have opened himself up to the risk of being pulled from 'pillar to post' within an embryonic function with very few boundaries or established relationships.

The inner certainty and anchorage that was provided by his own sense of purpose really mattered. It informed how he was showing up and his ability to influence key decision-makers with this new concept of how to drive growth. His clarity, confidence and ability to inspire others and bring them onboard was critical to the success of this new venture.

The classic phrase from the airline industry is very appropriate – it's vital to help the individual put his or her own 'oxygen mask' on first.

Does leadership enable the system or disable it?

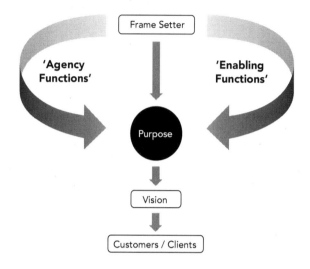

Another important aspect that enables orientation and provides individuals with a robust and reliable sense of place, is a clear flow of leadership.

This is about providing clarity on the context and enabling each part of the organisation to understand its function in service of the overall system. A clear flow of leadership provides a context within which everyone has a voice, understands what decisions are made where, and can do their work whilst growing and developing in a system that can flow and evolve.

The visual above demonstrates the archetypal setup of a leadership team, whereby the frame setter for the system (often the role of CEO or MD) is at the centre, facing the purpose of the business with the vision of the business and customers/clients/beneficiaries in their line of sight.

The optimum scenario is that to either side of the frame setter, you will have two types of functions, based on the roles they 'play' for the system.

From a systemic point of view, we call those functions which are externally facing and creating new business opportunities, the functions of 'agency'. Examples of agency functions include sales and marketing.

On the other side of the frame setter, the functions which enable the rest of the business to do their best work with customers and society, can be categorised as enablers. Without the enabling functions, the service to customers/clients and business opportunities would simply not be possible. Examples of enabling functions would include operations, logistics, HR and facilities, for example.

Both aspects are vital and are required for the overall business to function at its optimum. In a healthy system, each function understands where it fits, how it contributes and there is mutual respect of the contribution from the other. Everyone understands where and how decisions are made and what needs to be escalated vs what can sit within the scope of the parts.

> In a healthy organisation, there is energy, vitality and a capacity to sense and respond to impulses in the wider environment

Within healthy organisations, there is a clear sense of purpose and a clear flow of leadership. Each function takes its full place, no more and no less. When done well, each element of the business feels valued for its contribution to the whole and there is no need for internal competition.

The flow of leadership can easily get distorted during times of significant change such as in the case of mergers or acquisitions, when there are typically more decision-makers than there are decision-making roles.

Client example

"How can we position the integration of this acquisition without losing momentum of performance?", was the core question being posed by an established leader who had been given the task of bringing two separately managed parts of the business together.

Rob was renowned for his energetic leadership and driving performance across multiple geographies. The global leadership team were preparing Rob for his longer-term career trajectory and as part of this, had just given him the responsibility for integrating an organisation that had been acquired some years before, into the existing business. It was a complex and sensitive challenge that would develop his leadership to the next level.

This acquired company had a different, but complementary product range. It was of huge scale and as such, had been 'left' to operate separately with a business-as-usual mindset, by the global organisation for the first few years.

This included having its own central services and relevant cost centres. Within each business, there was a clear flow of leadership – everyone understood the core purpose, their place and their contribution to it, how decisions were made and the direction of travel.

Within the 'centre' the separation made sense, however, this construct created some confusion across most geographies. The reality of separate cost centres meant there were two leadership teams, making very different decisions (with distinctly different cultures and leadership styles) despite being co-located in the same building.

As is often the case, the need to drive efficiencies across the business came to the forefront of the agenda. It was decided to overtly integrate the two organisations to facilitate more cohesion and to realise some natural efficiencies.

The assumption at the start of this process was that the host business would assume responsibility for the acquired organisation and that employees of this acquired company would be superfluous to requirements in most cases. The projections on cost savings were calculated on this basis.

Rob was not comfortable with these projections or the assumed process.

As part of the coaching journey with Rob, he mapped this multidimensional system and the impact of the current structure became very evident, very quickly. In reality, this separation created confusion, frustration, duplication of effort and cost inefficiencies.

The original intention of allowing both parts to run independently was to provide freedom and maintain performance levels, however the opposite was being experienced in reality.

Within the various geographies, employees in the acquired business were concerned about following the strategic frame that was set by their leadership team, as they had an unspoken suspicion that it would be changed by the overall business anyway. In reality, the trust in leadership was eroded, energy was low and business performance was diluted at best.

Armed with the additional insight of how the system was operating, Rob set about the integration plan by involving both leadership teams – ensuring each had a voice. The starting place was to acknowledge all of the history and to leverage the combination of experience, expertise and sacrifices that were made to get to this juncture.

From here, they were able to reimagine the combined organisation, starting with purpose and how the business could serve its customers whilst continuing to evolve and grow.

Whilst the process of deciding upon the optimum structure and core leadership team was not an easy one, a more coherent flow of leadership was set in place.

Employees understood where each part fitted into the overall matrix, they understood where decisions were made or escalated to, which functions drove the business development and which parts enabled the organisation to deliver on its promise. They found a reliable place from which to make a meaningful contribution and felt acknowledged for it. Energy and performance flowed.

The systemic insights gathered throughout the process heavily influenced the change of journey and the communication throughout. Rob was able to identify what needed attention as he steered the integrated business back to healthy performance.

In summary

When the symptoms within the system are causing dysfunction and frustration is heightened, it's very easy to get pulled into the current narrative. You will be far more helpful to your coaching client, and to the system overall, if you can zoom back and wide, look for the repeating patterns, stay curious and free of judgment.

The root cause isn't always obvious or available on the surface and most of the time, there are a myriad of issues intertwined. These repeating patterns are operating at an unconscious level and you will need to review what has happened beyond the current time horizon.

The fundamental principles outlined within these first two chapters can provide a helpful reference for decoding the dynamics and getting to the root cause. It's only when you arrive there that you have a chance of sustainable breakthrough.

PERCOLATIONS...

As you look at the organisation you are working with OR working within, here's some provocation to keep in mind:

To what extent is there vitality and flow?

Can the system evolve and move?

Where (and at what moment in time) is it stuck?

What are the repeating patterns and where are they showing up?

Is the history (and all those who have significantly contributed to it) fully included and acknowledged?

Is there avoidance of the difficulties, pain points or consequences?

Who is 'turning away' from who/what?

Is there a balance of giving and taking (internally & externally)?

Can everyone find their place?

Do people feel like they belong?

How clear is the purpose?

Does leadership enable or disable the system?

CHAPTER THREE

DISRUPT THE LIMITING PATTERNS

Let's just remind ourselves that the role of the coach is to create movement in two key phases. Phase one is about identifying and releasing any limiting patterns and the second is about helping the client engage with, and step into, their full potential.

The precursor for movement is to increase the client's awareness of their own unconscious limiting patterns, and those of the multidimensional systems they are operating within

What is a limiting pattern?

What do I mean by a limiting pattern? In this context, I refer to a pattern of behaviour that repeats, without any logic or conscious awareness of why it is that way.

It may be the behaviour of the client themselves or it could be circumstances in the wider environment that they are affected by. In both cases, it is something that is happening in the here and now and on the face of it, it just doesn't make sense.

Inherent limiting patterns in the business might be due to unresolved dynamics further up the organisation or unresolved events sitting within its history. These unresolved issues/events are due to distortion or disruption in the fundamental principles of order, orientation and openness referenced in chapter 1. These may be from within the system or between the organisation and its wider ecosystem.

The other aspect to bear in mind, is that individuals may be carrying patterns from their personal system with them and if they have unresolved dynamics from this context, these will often be triggered and 'playing out' in the organisational setting.

The individual's unresolved family patterns can be playing out within the organisational context, without them realising it

---

I often use the analogy that each of us has two interconnected butterfly wings on our back, whereby one of the wings is influenced by our family system and the other by the organisational system that we belong to.

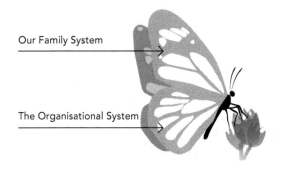

Our Family System

The Organisational System

It is not unusual for individuals to be unconsciously attracted to a role because of the hidden patterns that are active within the role or the organisation.

At some level, potentially due to their personal history, these dynamics are familiar and that familiarity breeds comfort. Put simply, systemic patterns in the organisation can attract individuals with similar patterns in their personal system.

The role of the coach

As the coach, distinguishing between the patterns of the client's personal system and that of the organisational context is incredibly important – we'll pick this up again later.

A big proportion of my coaching with leaders is to help them realise that they will, from time to time, collapse these two contexts together. The role of the coach is to raise the individual's awareness of this phenomenon and with this increased awareness, build the skill of separating these contexts.

The ideal of course, from a whole person perspective is that the client is open to working through these personal dynamics so as to sustainably release the limiting patterns for the long term. If you are an external coach and have the experience and skill, then this may be part of your remit. If you are an internal coach you will need to contract with the individual for this and if you are the line manager, then it might be about referring your direct report to an appropriately qualified professional.

When the coaching journey is activated, it is often because the impact of a limiting pattern has become amplified to an extent that something needs to change. This may not necessarily be seen or experienced as dysfunctional per se, nevertheless, limiting patterns can potentially sabotage one's life experience and leadership brand.

Traditional leadership coaching will often set about identifying the new behaviours that are required from the individual, supported by core values and beliefs. The coach will help the client start the journey of developing this clarity and whilst this endeavor is important and will, in time, be essential, in isolation, it will generally not be enough to enable sustainable change.

It's critical to get to the root cause of the limiting pattern, otherwise the pattern will just find another way or place to surface

How do limiting patterns form?

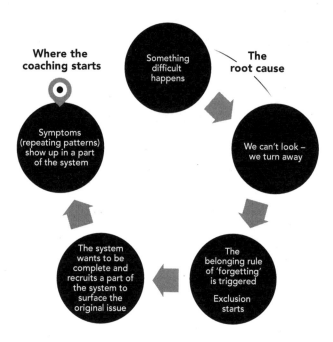

Limiting patterns form when something really difficult happens. As a way of surviving and staying in the system, i.e. maintaining

their fundamental sense of belonging, people look away from the difficult incident because it is too confronting.

As an example, if someone significant is exited from the business under a veil of secrecy or silence, everyone knows what has happened but have silently agreed to look away.

This event becomes a part of the history that is too difficult to talk about, and so it metaphorically slips into the shadows. It is simply too painful to look at the reality of what has happened at that point in time. And so, the belonging rule of not talking about it, of looking away, starts in that system – and so the exclusion begins.

As mentioned in chapter 1, the survival mechanism of the collective is to be complete. In this endeavour, the system will find a way of remembering the parts or experiences that were excluded. In this search for completeness, dynamics will continue to surface through a variety of routes.

These dynamics can show up through an individual or at a functional level and may not be a positive experience for either party! The wider system will sacrifice the individual for the sake of the whole but with this approach, you can intervene such that the individual does not have to be sacrificed.

Regardless of how it is showing up, it will keep repeating until it gets the attention that is required.

The overall process

As mentioned previously, we often need to go back in order to move forwards. We need to zoom back, stay curious and hold a stance that is free of judgment. The following process will provide some navigation through the complexity of limiting patterns, find their root cause and ultimately enable the system to settle and create movement towards the highest potential.

Honouring history and surfacing the pattern

You need to go back in order to move forwards. You need to get to the root cause or event where the distortion or disruption in the fundamental principles took place. By including these, you will be able to bring the unconscious, limiting patterns to the surface, appreciate their function and put them in context.

Your task is to get beneath and beyond the patterns in an effort to enable all parts of the system to settle and transform.

It is important to remember and acknowledge that these limiting patterns have served the individual, and the system at some level. That might only be to bring something from the wider system to the surface, for attention by the client or the organisation.

This is the stage when the primary and source events are exposed and the whole truth is revealed. These are often events that no one has dared to look at. There may be feelings of guilt and shame and can, therefore, be a moment of high vulnerability and a sense of feeling exposed. This is one of the reasons why creating the safe container at the outset is critical.

Acknowledge what is

Acknowledging what is, is one of the most crucial and settling parts of the systemic coaching process

The importance of dedicating time to acknowledging what is cannot be overstated. It is important not to rush this stage in the process – it allows space for the exposed source event to be respectfully explored, as appropriate, acknowledged and fully understood.

Once the patterns and their intention have been surfaced, the gifts that have been harvested need to be acknowledged and claimed. On face value, the experience of living with the patterns may not seem like a gift, but they can include learnings, insights and are also likely to include attributes or skills that have been developed.

It isn't always easy for the client to fully acknowledge and accept the gifts, but it is important that they are fully claimed before releasing the limiting pattern. If this isn't done well, an unhelpful attachment to what has been, remains at some level. At an energetical level, part of them will be left behind.

Creating movement

When we have given enough space to fully acknowledge the limiting pattern, exposing and understanding its intentions and harvesting the gifts, the pattern can be released and a readiness for movement is made possible.

Movement is enabled through a combination of sentence work and physical movement. Both can be deployed in a face-to-face setting or virtually.

There are specific sentences that can be utilised at each stage of the process above, and you will find an introduction to these within chapter 8, which is dedicated to the process of releasing the limiting patterns.

Earlier in this chapter, I referenced the importance of distinguishing between the personal system of the client and the organisational dynamic. Whilst the interventions may be similar in nature, it's important that we are doing the work in the right system and at the right level. We will come back to this in the next chapter.

The most prevalent limiting patterns

The patterns below are not an exhaustive list, but are those that you are most likely to come across in the organisational context. As mentioned previously, it is important to bear in mind that they may also be rooted in the personal system of the client.

The client examples that are included here describe the classic symptoms of each pattern and hopefully demonstrate how these patterns manifest in the organisational context.

Context overlay

Understanding this dynamic is probably one of the most important within this list of systemic patterns. It is one of the most prevalent patterns I observe with coaching clients and learning to recognise it, and work with it, will be of huge value within the individual and group coaching environment.

This pattern is about two contexts being unconsciously collapsed together without the individual (or group) realising it. This might be two separate layers from within the organisational context.

For example, when a restructure communication is being shared, the experience of a previous traumatic restructure scenario floods the conversation and is being projected into the current context. It can also involve a personal context being collapsed and projected in front of the current organisational scenario.

The signal that this pattern might be happening is when the level of emotional charge is significantly higher than that which is warranted by the current context.

The role of the coach in this scenario is to help the client separate the two contexts and realise that they are indeed, different. From there, you can help the individual work through whichever context is most appropriate at that point in time.

Client Example

"Am I really the kind of leader that is shutting people down? Am I creating a fear of speaking up? This is not the kind of leadership I recognise in myself. This is not who I want to be." This was the puzzle that Jack was trying to understand.

Jack was excited about his new three-year assignment. Although he was originally from Britain, he had spent most of his career based in several European locations and was in the early stages of developing his new leadership team in a large manufacturing business, headquartered in the US.

His regional leadership team were all US nationals and most of them had been in the team for some time. Jack was the newest member of the team and the only non-US national. This was an unusual phenomenon in itself, but it didn't concern Jack as he was used to working with lots of nationalities over the course of his career.

There were some classic reasons for a team development workshop which included two new members who had joined the team in the previous quarter and as a business, they were coming to the end of one business cycle and preparing for the next. In addition, and at the forefront of Jack's mind, the business was underperforming against expectations and Jack had a sense that the team were holding back but couldn't get to the bottom of why this was the case.

Jack was a highly consultative leader and his track record was paved with stories of creating healthy ecosystems that enabled constructive debate en route to robust decision-making. He had prioritised one-to-one time with this new team and believed he had established good relationships and the foundations of trust, but also believed there was something else going on which he couldn't quite put 'his finger on'.

Part way into the first day of the two-day team offsite, the pattern revealed itself. Each time the conversation was opened up for input, the team were tentative at best and in general, waiting to hear from Jack before they followed in line with his thinking. There weren't any new or alternative views coming from the team.

Some of this tentativeness might be explained by the cultural differences, but Jack had a strong sense that it was more than this. They seemed fearful but it didn't make any logical sense as to why that might be the case, given Jack's approach and their individual relationships with him thus far.

At an appropriate and relatively early stage in the session, and as part of honouring the history of the team and the business, the team was invited to create a 'history wall'. This provided them with some space and a framework to zoom back and take stock and leverage the experience of where the organisation had come from.

This included creating a timeline that acknowledged the initiation of the US business, key events, products and services, and key people that influenced the business along the way.

There was a three-year gap on the team's timeline that was almost empty of activity – it was almost as if this period of time didn't happen. From a systemic perspective, this can be an obvious indicator of some trauma in the system.

When the team were invited and encouraged to speak to this gap, it became evident that this was the last time the team had a Brit leading the team. This previous British leader had initiated significant unannounced restructures which had a direct impact on the leadership team in place at the time.

Because of the proposed direct impact on the individuals concerned, the incumbent leadership team had not been proactively consulted or engaged in the process at the time and as a result, these changes came as a significant shock.

A few members of the existing team had lived through this experience and a few of them had been exited in this period, only to be brought back into the business by the leader that followed. The root cause of the fear and shutting down was surfacing.

It became obvious that the systemic pattern of context overlay was at play. The team were unconsciously laying the previous context (British leader coming into the US and making drastic changes without appropriate consultation and communication) on top of the current context. They were projecting a highly charged experience onto Jack and their expectation of his leadership assignment.

As part of remembering, including and honouring the history, the truth was fleshed out and an acknowledgement of what really happened, and its impact, was shared.

This was not about making the history or previous leaders wrong or getting pulled into judgment, but it was about acknowledging how difficult this experience was for members of the team and how the ordering principles of mutuality and inclusion had been disrupted.

Acknowledging what is, is one of the most fundamentally healing and settling stages and creates the capacity for movement.

These first two crucial steps (honouring history and acknowledging what is) enabled the team to settle and the tentativeness to dissolve. This created the capacity for the different contexts to be seen as separate and the unconscious pattern of context overlay released. The team were freed up to bring their full selves and their valuable and insightful contributions to the conversation.

Identification

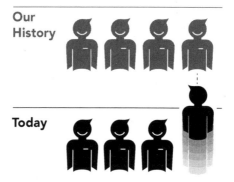

This is the dynamic whereby individual roles, functions or divisions are identified with a particular person, function, or unresolved issue which is typically from the past. There is an unconscious loyalty to something or someone, often triggered because it/they have been excluded.

This issue is often embedded in the history of the organisation, but it can also be triggered by events further up the hierarchy of the organisation. The current incumbents are not fully in the here and now – part of their energy and behaviour is caught up in a dynamic that is reminiscent of what is missing or being excluded, regardless of whether they knew them or knew about this previously.

> When someone or something significant is excluded, the system will find a way of pulling something or someone into the void

When an issue has been unresolved or excluded, the wider system will throw up the issue for attention by triggering dynamics in a part of the organisation such that they demand attention. The current incumbents are simply symptom bearers in the same way that within a family system, unresolved issues within the parents will show up as symptoms in the children.

For example, if a section of the business has been on the receiving end of a challenging series of exits that have not been handled with mutual respect and appropriate communication, it is very likely that another part of the business, e.g. the function that had to absorb the resulting overflow of workload, may not be able to operate at its optimum yet perhaps not understand why at a logical level.

Classic symptoms of this pattern include the client repeatedly experiencing feelings that are more representative of the parts or people that have been excluded. In the example above, this may manifest as a feeling of wanting to follow those that have been exited.

At some level, they feel guilty for the loss experienced by their previous colleagues and a way of staying connected with them is to energetically (and unconsciously) also 'check out' of the organisation and work at a level below par.

Another classic signal of identification is a sense of fixation, whereby the person (or function) is compelled to look at that which management can't. Through this fixation, they are drawing attention to what needs to be remembered.

It is not unusual for organisations to put all their attention on the actual part that is perceived as dysfunctional or operating below par and try to fix it or them. If it is at an individual level, then performance management or traditional coaching may be deployed.

If it is a function or division, the business may assume it is a leadership issue, at which point leaders may be changed or restructuring might be initiated.

If the source of the issue is indeed systemic, then none of these more 'traditional' or reactive approaches will create a long-term, sustainable shift. The pattern will repeat until the source event/ issue is surfaced, fully acknowledged and remembered.

Once the source event can be seen and fully acknowledged, the system and all its parts, especially those parts that were entangled in the identification dynamic, can settle and get back into a healthy flow.

This pattern of identification can be happening at an individual level (in someone's personal system) or within the organisational context and often, there can be a relationship between both of these dimensions.

Client Example

"What is wrong with me – why can I not take my place?" Aruna had tried everything obvious. Deep in her gut, she knew that she was capable. She needed to get to the truth.

We introduced Aruna earlier. She had recently come back from maternity leave to head up the highest revenue-generating division of the business and take her first seat in the leadership team. This division was responsible for over 30% of the overall revenue but had been experiencing a decline over the previous 18 months.

The key theme that was coming out of her stakeholder feedback was that she wasn't fully taking her place 'at the table' – 'she wasn't pulling her weight'. At a behavioural level, this showed up as holding back, not contributing to the conversation and behind the scenes, she was questioning herself on everything and asking her peers for their advice on what she should do with her business challenges. She was being indecisive.

On face value, it seemed to be a confidence issue. Her peers were starting to question her ability to steer their most important division out of a turndown and the general manager's decision to promote her was under scrutiny.

When the layers were peeled back on the personal aspect of Aruna's history, we discovered that Aruna was identified with her maternal grandmother. Based on her heritage and the family dynamic at the time, Aruna's grandmother could not find her place in her family of origin. She was always on the edge, invited in, but never really making that step, she was outside of the family circle and constantly felt separate and excluded.

The behavioural patterns witnessed in Aruna were remarkably similar to the grandmother she was clearly identified with. This was Aruna's unconscious way of staying in connection and the system's way of keeping the grandmother included. The collective conscience of the system will constantly seek ways of bringing back wholeness.

From a systemic perspective, Aruna was operating out of 'blind loyalty' to her grandmother, and by operating like her grandmother, i.e. staying on the outside periphery of things, Aruna was also not taking her full place within the leadership team or within her own team.

When this could be exposed for what it was, without judgment, Aruna was able to be released from this limiting pattern and freed up to remember and include her grandmother in a more conscious and helpful way.

Releasing these dynamics takes some time to settle and for the limiting pattern of behaviour to dissipate. When the client has had time to integrate the work undertaken, they often report a strong sensation of feeling lighter and freer to move forward.

In Aruna's case, within nine months she went on to become one of the strongest members of the leadership team and won a global award for her masterful turnaround of the division. This was a whole person intervention and as such, she experienced the positive ripple effects in her personal life too!

Distortions of place

When there is a void at the levels above, it is easy to get pulled out of your 'right' place and into the vacuum. Something is missing and the system will seek to find something or someone to fill the gap. This is as true in the organisational system as it is in the family setting.

If this pattern is active in your personal family system, then you are more likely to be predisposed for recruitment into this vacuum within the organisational context. If this is familiar territory for you, then you are ripe for recruitment! It is vital to emphasise that none of this is happening at a conscious level and there are consequences both positive and limiting.

Whilst there are some inherent gifts that can be harvested from this distortion of place, it is not a sustainable way of operating in the longer term. It involves carrying more responsibility than is yours to carry and over time, this will feel burdensome, and the individual may, in time, experience burnout or feel resentful.

There are two main variations of this distortion of place, as follows:

Triangulation

Triangulation involves being pulled 'one level up' in the hierarchy

Within the organisational context, triangulation would manifest as a direct report being pulled up to the same level as the line manager.

This will happen when someone or something is missing at the manager level. The manager is potentially seeking a sounding board and unconsciously pulls someone 'up' to their level for discussion, sharing and ideation.

Ultimately it involves a direct report being inflated beyond their position and although they will have stepped up with good intention, the phenomenon is likely to trigger negative reactions from their peers and the wider team.

This will not be a conscious decision for either party. For the manager it's based on the fact that something is missing and on the part of the triangulated individual, they act out of a desire to help.

Whilst it is an unconscious manoeuvre, in the long term it is not healthy for either party. The triangulated individual can end up feeling exhausted by trying to fill the gap in addition to doing their actual role, and also feel like they are not quite in either position fully, i.e. they are neither a peer or a direct report. This can also cause confusion, and over time, tension in the relationship between the line manager and the inflated direct report.

There are some gifts of being triangulated. They include the development of the ability to attune to others and from that increased sensitivity, anticipate the needs of more senior stakeholders and clients.

Client example

"I'm excluded from most things. They don't involve me, I don't feel like I belong here, and it hurts. Why does this keep happening to me?" lamented Jemma in one of our early coaching sessions.

Jemma had worked her way up through her specialist profession – she was a HR expert and had gathered her experience across a range of organisations and industry sectors. When I started working with her, she had HR responsibility for the largest division within a global engineering business, based in Europe.

She already had a couple of senior leadership roles 'under her belt' and in this quest to gather global experience, Jemma had moved companies and countries every two or three years. She was originally from the US but had worked extensively across Europe. Her ambitions were to progress to take responsibility for HR on a global scale.

There was no question on her professional capabilities. However, in terms of relationships, things were a little bit more complex. With regard to relationships with her leadership colleagues from the other functions, she could never quite find her 'right place'. She felt that she didn't quite fit in and often felt excluded from conversations/decisions/meetings.

She realised, on a logical level, this would not have been a conscious decision on the part of her colleagues, nevertheless it was a repeating pattern that she had been experiencing beyond the current organisation.

Her relationship with her functional line manager (the global CHRO) was tense. There was an unspoken tussle with regard to boundaries – Jemma felt that the global CHRO was often stepping into her territory and when stakeholder feedback was sourced, the same was perceived the other way around.

When peeling back the layers of Jemma's personal family system, it was discovered that she was the only child of a single mother.

In this family setting, she was often 'pulled up' into the place of the mother's partner and confidante. When someone is 'pulled up' to the next level (in this case, to the vacuum left by her missing father), they are pulled into a place that is 'too big'.

Jemma was in adult conversations long before her time and to some extent, learned how to sit alongside her seniors as an equal rather than in the place of the child. She was pulled up and operating one level above her right place in her family system – she was triangulated.

As a consequence of this experience in her personal system, Jemma was predisposed to being recruited into similar scenarios in other settings including her work environment.

At an unconscious level, her internal position was about operating alongside the global CHRO as an equal, as opposed to operating as a direct report. None of this would have been intentional of course, but it was playing out in their working relationship.

Peers felt she kept herself separate and that she gravitated to the more senior stakeholders, and in response, started to exclude her. There was an unspoken sense that she seemed to think she was 'above everyone else', and her exceptional business results only amplified this perception.

Her boss was getting exasperated, and the perceived lack of respect was creating significant tension. Despite delivering results that were beyond expectations, Jemma found herself feeling exposed, undervalued and at risk should further restructuring come onto the global agenda.

On face value, helping Jemma agree and set boundaries and ways of working with her colleagues and her boss would be a credible component of this coaching assignment.

However, until this systemic limiting pattern of triangulation and the root cause from her personal system was fully exposed, acknowledged and dealt with, Jemma's inner and inflated unconscious position of operating 'one level up' would only surface again.

As per the overall process mentioned earlier, step one is to help the individual honour their history, surface the limiting pattern and its root cause without judgment, to fully acknowledge the consequences and harvest the gifts. From here, the readiness for movement is activated.

Parentification

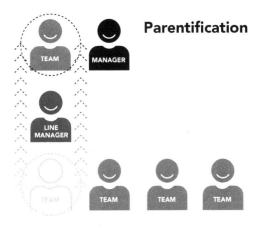

Parentification is about being pulled two levels up

Within the organisational context, this means that an individual is pulled into the vacuum above their line manager. When senior leadership is missing, individuals (and sometimes whole functions), with the very best of intentions, are recruited into the vacuum and end up in the inflated position of managing their manager.

Within the family setting, this is about parenting your parents, i.e. taking the place of the grandparent which can often be required during times of serious illness.

If someone is parentified in their personal system, they are a prime candidate for being recruited into this pattern within the organisational setting.

As is the case with each of these patterns, this is not a conscious choice of behaviours. The essence of the parentified individual is one of perceived arrogance. They feel more equipped to deal with situations than their line manager and can therefore appear disrespectful. They may find accepting authority from others difficult and may prefer to have control or to step out of the system in order to take control of their own destiny.

It is important to note that there are also gifts to be harvested before releasing this pattern. In the case of parentification, the primary gift is that of being willing to take responsibility, to carry the load.

Parentified individuals tend to be resilient, they have a strong degree of self-reliance and are resourceful. Because they readily and often proactively take on more responsibility, they may find themselves climbing the career ladder quickly, however, they may also find themselves in burnout.

Client Example

"I'm the only one who sorts things out around here – you can't rely on anyone else. How can they let me go?" was the frustration and confusion expressed by Magdalene.

Magdalene found herself exited from her organisation and didn't really understand why. She was a senior HR professional with decades of experience behind her. She had worked in various locations including the UK, Europe and the US and for the first time in her career, she found herself with the tables turned and on the receiving end of an exit package with nowhere to go.

She had not been happy for a while. Picking up the responsibility for the various change initiatives before they collapsed was a familiar pattern. Her manager was too busy and as far as Magdalene was concerned, her peers were not competent enough. Their attention to detail was not at the level it needed to be and from her perspective, no one else really understood the full implications of what needed to be done and when.

Magdalene felt that she had been doing all the heavy lifting and felt deeply hard done by. She found herself wondering what had happened. It was time to have a good look at what was going on.

Upon review of her career journey, she unpacked her history on a timeline and realised that this pattern of taking over, grabbing responsibility for the critical tasks in the major projects and viewing most others as incompetent, had been running for some time. This could not be a coincidence!

When reviewing her personal history, it became evident very quickly that she was parentified in her family system. She was the only child of divorced parents and was pulled into the role of mediator, and an emotional crutch for one of her parents, from a very young age.

At an unconscious level, she was pulled up into the inflated role of parenting one of her parents and had quickly learned how to take control, be self-sufficient and not trust others to share the load.

Magdalene was a prime candidate for being recruited into the vacuum left by the absence of leadership within the organisational setting.

She acted with good intention, deep care and a desire to help. Over time, Magdalene took on the unconscious belief that they, i.e. everyone else, was incapable of doing things properly and she would just take control, to the point where everyone stood back and let her get on with it.

This pattern of taking the bigger place had translated into the organisation as arrogance and independence. She was not perceived as a team player or a collaborator. So when the function was being transformed, she was a prime candidate for an exit package despite being one of the most experienced and relied-upon members of the team.

The coaching focus for Magdalene was about helping her to see the pattern, where it came from and its impact. Ultimately, it involved gradually learning to respectfully acknowledge and leverage the expertise and experience of others and learn how to stay in her right place.

As part of this, it was important to nurture enough systemic awareness around the potential triggers so that she would know how to refrain from being pulled out of her right place again.

Polarisation

Let's think about this from a personal dimension to start with. When we are polarised, we inhabit a part of ourselves and disown the other part. There is a split.

There's a part that we feel comfortable with. We find this other dimension repulsive and have a tendency to feel better than it. The reality however, is that both parts exist and we actually also embody this 'other part' without realising it.

The area that has been most explored with regard to this systemic pattern is the polarity of victim and perpetrator. What we know is that each victim also embodies the essence of the perpetrator, i.e. their behaviour in some aspect of their life embodies perpetrator energy. The same is true the other way around. This duality is outside of our conscious awareness.

The pattern of polarisation is calling attention to the fact that both parts want to come together and reconcile a split that has happened further back in time. This split is often nothing to do with the person/function through whom the polarisation is showing up.

When the pattern is playing out, it can feel impossible to reconcile these two parts. However, once we can acknowledge and integrate both parts, we can move beyond the polarity.

This enables the individual/function to be freed up from the dynamic of feeling pulled and repulsed by either end of the spectrum. When both parts are integrated, it enables the individual/function to be right-sized, i.e. everything is back in perspective and the individual (or function) is not better or worse than the rest.

This pattern can also show up in the organisational setting. This may show up as workers vs management or region vs headquarters. As we know, each of these elements is needed to make a stronger organisation.

In addition, some of the classic situations where this dynamic may be further triggered include restructures, redundancies, mergers and acquisitions.

The intervention that interrupts this pattern and helps the individual/function to grow beyond it, starts with zooming back. This enables the client to comprehend when/where the split happened, to see a larger context, within which both ends of the spectrum can, and do exist.

It is about helping them to see the broader perspective and that it doesn't have to be an 'either or'. It is also about recognising that there is a broader context within which each polar opposite, in fact, needs the other to be complete.

....

ONE STEP

It's too much, too big, too vast – I hear myself say – there's so much to do

I need to move fast – to make a leap – I have to jump

My body and mind are all stirred up – I'm getting ready to run

But it's too much – it's overwhelming

So I shrink back to where I was and I don't move

I'm caught up in the shall I or shall I not?

Time to go OR shall I wait for a while?

I'll wait for the right moment – the sign that it is the right time

I'm caught up in the illusion of a perfect move

I'm stuck in the vacuum of unused energy, unused movement – it's draining me

This polarising pattern of move and don't move yet, needs to be released – to be given back

Who owns this?

To whom am I being loyal by keeping this alive within me?

And then the mist lifts – there's a bigger context beyond me

Where two parts were split

....

....

Where this tussle belongs and makes perfect sense

And when this can be seen and acknowledged, I'm released

I'm no longer caught up in that 'in between' place

Standing in someone else's shoes

Of wanting to move, but not moving – frozen

My One Step is a step of the right size – the footprint that comes from MY feet

This 'One Step' is not about holding two sides separately

Or paying a price

It's for me

It's coming from me

It's the right size

At last I can breathe

And I can move forward again

One Step at a time

....

Summary

Our role as coach is to help raise the client's awareness of the limiting patterns that are active and their source. We need to discern whether the patterns are from the client's personal system or from their organisational context. Keep in mind that patterns in the organisational context often attract and activate similar patterns within the client.

There is an extensive spectrum of limiting patterns and within this chapter we have covered those that you are most likely to encounter within an organisational context.

- **Context overlay** – where there is another context unconsciously laid in front of the current reality.

- **Identification** – roles, functions or divisions are identified with a particular person, function, or unresolved issue which has been excluded.

- **Triangulation and parentification** – these are distortions of place, whereby individuals (or functions) are pulled one or two levels up and out of their right place in the organisation.

- **Polarisation** – a sense of being split between two parts that need to be reconciled and integrated.

When awareness is activated and the impetus for change is high, we can help the client break free from these patterns by acknowledging the root cause and allowing the disruptions and distortions of the fundamental principles covered earlier to be addressed.

You will often discover that a complex combination of limiting patterns and symptoms have been triggered within the system. It's helpful to remember that you sometimes need to go back in order to go forwards. The systemic process below provides a route map to follow.

PERCOLATIONS...

Take some time to review your own limiting patterns as a coach, and where relevant, in your leadership. It's not unusual for our own patterns to be showing up in how we approach our client and their system. An acute level of self-awareness through doing 'our own work' is a prerequisite for offering this approach to others.

1. What are your own repeating patterns?

2. Where/what might the root cause of these be?

3. How has this liming pattern served you, until now? What gifts can you harvest?

4. If we assume it is trying to tell you something about your own system, what is it drawing your attention to?

5. What needs to be acknowledged and included so that you can be set free?

CHAPTER FOUR

GET TO THE ROOT CAUSE

Survival Mechanisms

When navigating through the complexity of limiting patterns, to get to the root cause, it's helpful to bear in mind the three survival mechanisms we mentioned within chapter 1.

The individual dimension

At the individual dimension we are working with the core survival mechanism of the need to belong. A lot of what is going on is happening at a conscious level. Individuals, driven by the fear of being excluded, will make sacrifices around some of the most fundamental principles in order to fit in.

By individual, we are referring to one part of the system. This can be a specific role, a team, a function or a division within a wider organisation.

The collective dimension

At the collective dimension, we are working with the whole system and its innate and ongoing desire for completeness. The survival mechanism is a drive for wholeness.

When key events or parts (people or functions) are excluded, limiting patterns will be triggered in the system. These limiting patterns are channelled through parts of the system. Importantly, the relevant individuals or groups are not consciously aware of them.

The function of the limiting patterns is to draw attention to the unresolved issues of previous generations and confront the current incumbents until they are surfaced and settled and will repeat until this happens.

The wider system always takes precedence over the individual dimension and will often sacrifice the parts in service of facilitating wholeness.

A classic example of the system sacrificing an individual for the sake of the whole is the repeating pattern called 'the ejector seat'.

This refers to a role in the organisation that keeps churning through really good people despite leading-edge recruitment systems and top talent being employed. It is easy to make an instant judgment that the issue is with the individual.

It is more helpful to suspend this assumption and check how long the phenomenon has been recurring in the context of the specific role in question. If it is a repeating pattern, then you are more likely to be dealing with a distortion or disruption of one of the order principles (time, exchange, place and belonging) that has not yet been addressed.

Repeating limiting patterns suggests that there is a
distortion or disruption of the ordering principles

Something has happened further back in time, or further up the
organisation, that has been too difficult to confront and accept at
the time. And so, the limiting pattern is initiated.

The perfect role that can't be filled

An example of this came to light when I was facilitating a
team session for a major FMCG organisation, producing
household brands. They noticed that the president role for
the Asia Pacific region was causing major concern. As this
was a key region of growth, this was becoming a critical issue.

They had turned over three people in this leadership role
within 12 months despite the best recruitment process and
securing exceptionally strong talent. The leavers fed back
to the business that they felt they couldn't stay – always a
warning signal to take note of.

When the situation was unpacked from a systemic perspective,
the root cause became obvious very quickly. The original
setup of the region included two senior leadership roles, each
responsible for 50% of the region.

As part of a restructure, a decision was made to reduce the
leadership role to one. This happened quickly and without due
process or appropriate communication with the individuals
involved.

The ordering principle of mutuality between the organisation
and the exited employee was sacrificed for the sake of speed.
There was no explicit acknowledgement of the lack of process,

the contribution of the exiting individual to the business, or the consequent impact of this change on them or their team.

In fact, in the interests of speed and getting the region merged quickly, those remaining in the newly-merged region were not proactively engaged in the process either. There was no malice or negative intentions in this scenario, it was simply a judgment call by the leaders at the time, that prioritised speed above proactive communication and explicit acknowledgement.

The remaining leader who was allocated the role of the newly-combined region decided to leave after a few months – they could not stay because of an unconscious level of guilt. Their role was burdened and it was turning over good candidates ever since.

As this region was of strategic importance, a member of the executive leadership team wanted to get the recruitment issue of this key role resolved. As a consequence, an inquiry was set up to explore what might be happening from a systemic perspective.

We stepped back in time to get to the source event. The dynamic was showing up through the churn of this regional president role, but the source of the issue was further back in time. The systemic function of this limiting pattern was to bring the root cause to the surface.

The collective system (and those within it), needed an explicit acknowledgement of the lack of process, the deficit of mutual exchange and its impact, to enable the system to settle.

The current employees of the Asia Pacific region would not have been rationally aware of this need – this need to surface the root cause was sitting in the unconscious but making itself known nevertheless.

This combination of working at the right level and with the right individuals (those who were responsible for the overall system), meant that we were able to unburden the Asia Pacific president role, settle the system and ultimately enable performance breakthroughs and the growth trajectory to return.

The upcoming future

This final survival mechanism is the innate need to connect to something greater than self. When you are working with the evolutionary force of the upcoming future, you are trying to understand what is trying to flow. You are checking for the impulses for change that are emerging and what is needed for this flow to happen.

When working in this domain, the aim is to help the individual get into contact with the movement that is trying to come towards and flow through them.

What is often overlooked, but needs attention, is what needs to stop in order to create some space for the new to emerge.

Depending on how comfortable the individual is with endings – which can be uncovered through the exploration of their 'history' – you may need to support them with the endings aspect.

Is the seat fully available?

We met Laura back in chapter 2, where she was exploring her various career options through the systemic mapping process.

She uncovered two viable options that met the needs of her family and enabled her to live to her highest potential.

Laura felt a strong urge to move forward towards one of these opportunities but also detected a slight drag factor. She sensed something was holding her back and if this wasn't addressed, she may not be fully available to step into the new opportunity.

It is not unusual to find some hesitance on moving from job to job or company to company. From a systemic point of view, we put a lot of attention on good beginnings and healthy endings. We want to ensure that energetically, the individual doesn't leave parts of themselves behind but equally should also not bring things that belong to the old organisation with them.

The dimension of systemic ownership is important in this context – who owns what needs to be made explicit and honoured. In principle, things that have been created whilst under the employ of the organisation, belong to said company.

It is important to identify those things/products/ideas that have been created during the time of employment that technically belong to the current organisation – and to leave these behind for the organisation to do what they believe to be appropriate with these. It is particularly important to explicitly acknowledge that the outgoing individual has no further claim to them.

It is not unusual, especially when individuals have been in a role for a long time, that they leave parts of themselves behind.

It's equally important, therefore, to help the individual identify all those elements of themselves that they need to retrieve, including their energy, passion and expertise.

The combination of both aspects above ensures the exit is 'clean' and that the individual can bring all of their energy and attributes into their next opportunity. It also means that the role they are leaving behind is unencumbered. The endings process is important for both parties.

Working at the right level in the system

The overriding objective of systemic coaching is to facilitate movement so that the client (individual or a group) can deliver at the highest level of performance, whilst moving towards and occupying their full potential.

When you are working with multiple levels of the organisation, it is important to open up issues that are relevant and appropriate for the level of the specific individual client or team. By opening up issues that are destined for more senior levels of leadership, you parentify the client, i.e. make them too big and burden them with issues they cannot hold or affect. This is not healthy for them or for the wider system.

In order to facilitate a sustainable movement for the client, it's important to 'work' with the appropriate survival mechanism that has been activated. Bear in mind that you might need to work with all three mechanisms in stages over the course of the coaching journey.

Client example

"There's an underlying tension in the team but I can't quite get to the bottom of it."

Jemma had inherited a global team who had lived through several mergers and acquisitions. And whilst it was a very successful team, there were many examples of tension and a series of clashes between specific individuals. The dynamics were showing up between people from the various companies that had been brought together.

The narrative in the business was that these acquisitions enabled significant growth and accelerated the trajectory of the organisation, however the integration was not managed as well as it could have been.

Jemma was really frustrated, as she couldn't get to the bottom of the team dynamics – each time she thought she had dealt with the issue at hand, the tension popped up somewhere else.

She took the opportunity upon the appointment of one of her new managers to review the history with the wider team, as part of their onboarding process.

As it was a virtual event, they co-created a map of the history of the organisation on to a virtual whiteboard. This included positive and challenging experiences, significant milestones, business developments, key contributors and key events. They also mapped each person's arrival into the business and the team on to the timeline.

When they got to the key events around the mergers and acquisitions, tensions rose significantly and the unhealthy dynamics surfaced again.

From a systemic perspective, you look beyond the immediate symptoms and the individuals – you need to suspend judgment and get to the root cause.

Two very helpful questions to hold are:

1. What is the very good reason that this might be happening?

2. What is this dynamic trying to tell us?

Jemma asked each team member to share their personal experience of the merger/acquisition and started to understand the underlying issues.

She then invited the team to zoom back, take a wider lens and to identify the value that each of the companies brought to the overall business. This helped to ensure that exchange was made explicit and that each of the merged companies had its place in the overall system.

Finally, she ensured that each member of the team felt like they had been listened to, had clarity of their place in the team and that the place of the overall team was also clear in the wider context of the overall organisation.

As this intervention was not at the executive leadership team, it was not appropriate to review how the original integration of the acquisition was handled or to deal with any distortion of the ordering principles as part of that process – this would have been inappropriate. This would have made Jemma's team too big – it would have 'parentified' them in the system.

Summary

Your role is to get to the deeper reason as to why the situation is as it is now, i.e. to ascertain the systemic function of the repeating pattern and bring to the surface the underlying issues that need to be resolved. By doing so, you can facilitate accurate acknowledgement of what is, and enable the system to be settled and complete so that healthy movement can return.

Within a coaching context, creating an understanding of the client's journey to date, at both the personal and organisational dimensions will provide a lot of the information you are likely to require.

Bear in mind, however, that there may be a combination of these limiting patterns, fuelled by the survival mechanisms, happening in the wider organisation.

In order to get to the root cause, it's helpful to look through the lens of the ordering principles (time, place, mutual exchange and belonging), when you are exploring the history of the individual and the organisational context.

Taking your time, incorporating laser-like questions, multidimensional listening, trusting your intuition and staying free of judgment are critical components of the systemic approach.

It is not possible to change what has happened in the history of the system, but it is possible to explicitly acknowledge what has happened and change the relationship to it. Rather than keep turning away, what has happened can be acknowledged as part of the history, and a moment in time, from which lessons can be learned.

Finally, an important aspect to bear in mind when you are exploring the root cause, is that we need to be careful of what we are 'opening up' in terms of the history and what is happening within the various layers of the organisation. Only open things up that you know the client has permission to see.

To some extent the system will protect itself anyway. There is a view that the systemic layers will only show themselves to those who have permission to look and to those coaches and facilitators who are skilled enough to hold the process.

PERCOLATIONS...

1. What symptoms might trigger you into making instant assessments/judgments, rather than zooming back to look for the root cause?

2. When might you get pulled into should-dos of the planned future vs allowing the nudges from the more emergent, upcoming future to connect with you?

   a. What prompts or practices can you put in place for yourself and recommend to your clients, to listen more carefully to these nudges?

3. How comfortable are you with endings?

    a. What does this bring up/trigger for you?

    b. If there's work to be done on your own endings, it is worth giving some attention to this so that you can facilitate this process for others.

CHAPTER FIVE

THE HARNESS COACHING MODEL

HARNESS: To make use of natural resources to produce energy

After many years of integrating the systemic approach into my leadership coaching, the HARNESS framework emerged. I have found that it has helped me to stay clear and focused on where I am in the process of helping the client with the two key movements, mentioned earlier.

This systemic approach to leadership coaching has seven key phases. Each phase will need varying amounts of time and attention. It's important to say these aren't linear phases because there will be times when you need to go back and revisit and do more development work in some of the previous phases.

It's not unusual for a client to share information on a limiting pattern or express some degree of stuckness that didn't surface at the outset of the journey. This is just a signal that the client is ready and open for work in this area. I would take it as a compliment, in fact, that the container has been made safe enough for the client to be willing to go back and dig deeper.

Honouring history

The first of these phases is about making sure that everything that has happened up to this point, and those who have contributed to the current state, are fully included.

It involves gathering and honouring all of the history leading up to this point in time. From the organisational context, this includes the career trajectory thus far, experience and skills gathered along the way, challenges and pain points encountered and the gifts that have been harvested as a result.

The client's personal system is also important. It's supremely helpful to gather ancestral data beyond the immediate family system of the client. The ideal is to be able to go back three generations, as we know from research that repeating patterns can be carried through the family system for this duration.

Clearly, some upfront positioning will be required with the client so that they can be assured that all information will be handled with incredible care, sensitivity, and of course the utmost confidence. If you are working as an internal coach, creating a contract of confidentiality is critical. This first stage is about getting an understanding of everything that has happened (the good, the difficult and the painful) up to this point in time and including it.

Bearing in mind the essential foundations of a safe container, you might find that a more complete version of history unfolds over time. Work with what you have to start with and gradually build from there.

Acknowledge current reality

The second phase is about incorporating a sense of what is happening today. The recommendation is to engage the client's key stakeholders in this process and ideally on a 360-degree dimension, i.e. gather feedback from people working around them. This will include the line manager, second line manager, peers, direct reports (and a sample of layers below that, if this is relevant).

This provides a multilayered and a multidimensional perspective on how your client is showing up in their current reality. It ensures that the reality as other people see it, is included alongside the client's own perspective.

The conversations with stakeholders are designed to gather information on what is going well, what is diluting value, data on any repeating patterns, and insights on their perceived future potential.

Ultimately, this phase is about getting to the truth of where we are starting from and a reality check on their leadership brand from the outset.

Release limiting patterns

The third phase is uncovering and releasing the unconscious limiting patterns, and any related unhelpful strategies. There can often be a variety of limiting patterns that are active for the client and in the system within which they operate. The most prevalent ones are covered in chapter 3.

In order to release the limiting patterns, you must get to the root cause and be sure to get to the right level in the system and the right timeframe that the source event took place. When this can be fully included and acknowledged, you are ready to harvest the gifts that have been gained from carrying these patterns. This step is often forgotten and is important as you will want to resource the client as they move forward.

Nurture systemic awareness

Phase four is about nurturing systemic awareness. Whilst this is identified as a specific phase, the reality is that you are nurturing this capability the whole way through the coaching journey. Having mastered the first few phases, the client is typically ready for understanding a bit more of the process.

The intention is to help them build their understanding of this systemic perspective so that they are more aware of what triggers them and others, and from these triggers, be clearer on what belongs to them and what might belong to other people or the wider system.

Ultimately, this will enable them to better navigate the complexity and ambiguity that is their current reality.

Engage with the upcoming future

This is about helping the client to look beyond what they feel they should do or to fulfil a plan that was created many years previously. It might also help them move beyond any dimension of ego that is running their schedule. It's about helping them to connect and engage with a sense of what's calling, listening for what the world (or society) wants from them rather than what they are striving for from the world, or feel compelled to undertake, triggered by a sense of duty or loyalty.

The evolutionary force of the upcoming future is often suggesting it's time for something to stop and to make way for something else. This can include acknowledging something has reached its destiny and it's time to create space for what wants to flow, to emerge.

This is not necessarily an easy phase to navigate and may involve making some brave and conscious choices.

Strengthen the sense of purpose

From this position and with the stimulus of the upcoming future in mind, we can really start to help the client to create a sense of purpose. This provides a sense of orientation and has an anchoring effect for the individual and the organisation. When you are working one-to-one, it is recommended that you ensure the individual dimension has some solidity before adding the additional layer of the organisational purpose.

Within the context of this bigger why, they can also distil or refresh their leading principles. Leading principles help to clarify the hierarchy of things that really matter in the delivery of this purpose – I'll expand on this further within chapter 11.

Solidify leadership brand

The final phase is about spending some time in bringing everything that has been undertaken so far, together. The aim is to solidify their leadership brand by reviewing and finalising their sense of purpose, their leading principles, their core values, what behaviours people will see, and what behaviours people won't see.

This consolidation enables the client to respond to the following questions/provocations:

1. Who are you?

2. Why are you here?

3. What do you stand for?

4. What do you stand against?

5. What can people expect from you as a leader?

6. What do you need to operate at your best?

CHAPTER SIX

HONOUR HISTORY

....

THE STONE IN MY SHOE

The stone in my shoe is there as a constant

It rubs my skin from time to time

And it hurts.

The stone in my shoe is there as a constant

Sometimes it finds a new spot to settle into

And it's quiet for a while – not stirring

Until things are triggered, and then it makes itself known.

To be looked at – to be seen, and to be felt

And when I can acknowledge its presence,

And the gifts I have gained from carrying it

It can soften and melt back into the background

To become part of the fabric as opposed to separate from it.

No longer rubbing – but still present

....

No longer hurting – but still present

I honour this stone in my shoe

It has made me who I am and informed how I walk in the world

I am stronger for it – and I would be incomplete without it

It has become part of me – and I part of it

I stand more complete.

And yet, by acknowledging its part – I can also stand separate
from it

To look beyond the stone

To honour the rock from which it was birthed

The bigger system from which it came

It is much bigger than me and us

It too, deserves to be seen.

Honour and include history

As part of my own personal development journey, it took me some time to fully acknowledge and include my history and all that this entailed. When I realised that my history has made me who I am and provided many gifts, I could finally look at what was 'behind me', include it and reclaim it.

Up until that point, and from time to time, I would be triggered by the trauma and pain of my past. Like that tiny stone that I refer to in this poem, it can find its way into your shoe, and although incredibly small, it can be surprisingly painful.

Don't get pulled into the rush of fixing things – lean back

To provide ultimate value to your client, it's important not to be pulled into the urgency of what needs to change before acknowledging all of the history that has happened up to this point. History in this context takes into consideration all of the client's experience from their organisational context and their family heritage.

From the outset of the coaching programme, it's about gathering and honouring all that has happened in their journey and building up a context that helps makes sense of who they have become and why they show up the way that they do.

Your coaching client has many layers to them. There is complexity lying beneath the surface. Some of the patterns within this complexity come from their experience within the organisational context and some may be transferring across from their personal context.

Latest research in neuroscience has proven that traumatic experiences and stress reactions can travel through the genes for up to three generations such that symptoms show up in the great grandchildren even when they have had no direct experience or knowledge of the traumatic events of their ancestors. [3]

From a systemic perspective, this philosophy is not only relevant within the family context but also within the organisational setting. The organisation has been found to hold a memory that is beyond the individuals concerned at the time.

In order to enable a sustainable change, your first priority is to review this complexity and identify the patterns that have enabled their success thus far as well as those that may have reached their expiry date.

The most important thing to remember is that everything needs to be included within the history – it all belongs. You can't just dismiss or disregard the difficult or complicated elements. When you exclude, great experiences cannot be fully leveraged and the unresolved issues will keep repeating in various dimensions until they get the attention they require. When significant elements are excluded, energy and attention continue to look back rather than being free to look forward. This is often unconscious, of course.

When we can honour all of our history, we are stronger

Mapping the history

As the patterns that are active within the client can be rooted from either the family or organisational context, it's helpful to map both dimensions.

Their place in the family system came first in the order of time, so it might make sense to start there. You are aiming to gather information from a minimum of three generations on both sides of the family.

With regard to the organisational history, gather as much information about the organisation since it was founded as possible. If the client has only been there a short time, it is worth gathering some history on their previous organisation (and their journey within it) as well.

Look through the lens of the ordering principles we talked about in chapter 2 and in particular when these may have been distorted or disrupted. You are listening for repeating patterns.

Listen and tune in to moments in the story when the client is emotionally charged – these are situations to gently unpack and understand. Pay attention to your own energy and when this lifts and falls – be open to the fact that this is probably telling you something about the energy in their system. Don't ignore this – acknowledge what is happening within you. Pause in these moments to enquire – check if your sensations are familiar to them.

Here are some questions to hold when compiling the history map of both dimensions (personal and organisational) with your client:

1. What are the significant events that have informed the experience that exists today?

2. When were things at their most vibrant and energetic, and what enabled this?

3. How has any wealth been gathered?

4. To what degree is there a balance of give and take with the relevant parties/stakeholders?

5. Have there been any incidents when things got difficult/ stuck/became toxic, and if so, what happened?

6. Who are the significant people who have influenced things over time?

7. Is there anyone in history who is forgotten or not talked

about? And if so, what do we need to know about that?

8. What are the patterns that keep repeating?

Here are some of the elements that are informative to include in the history map:

Key events that have influenced the trajectory of each system

- Introduction of new brands, services, etc
- Early or tragic loss of life or closure of parts of the business
- Mergers, acquisitions, major restructuring, etc

Key people who have influenced things as they are today

- Within the maternal and paternal family context this will include parents (or carers), aunts, uncles, grandparents, great-grandparents, siblings (including siblings within blended families).

- Within the organisational context, this will include founders, and all individuals who have significantly influenced the organisation on its journey to date.

Key aspects relating to mutual exchange

- Where and how the family has earned (or inherited) their

income and to what degree there was mutual exchange within the family.

- Where and how the organisation was funded at the time of its origin and significant changes to the financing of the business, e.g. if the business ownership changes.

- How the organisation generates its income and if there is a healthy level of mutual exchange between the organisation and the employees.

- The balance of exchange between the organisation and its customers and suppliers.

Situations where the fundamental principles (3 x Os) have become disrupted or distorted

- Leadership has been missing at a certain level (or levels) and others keep getting unconsciously recruited into the vacuum, but later suffer the consequences.

- There are certain roles in the organisation that have a high churn – people don't seem to be able to settle – this is a classic symptom that there has been a disruption in the systemic ordering forces further back in time.

Zoom back together

When you have completed compiling the history map, take time to review this with the client. Ensure you both zoom back and as you do so, look for themes and repeating patterns.

Examples of these might be behaviours or dynamics that are very similar to ancestors or predecessors in the role/function or behaviours that seem like they are compensating for something that happened earlier in the timeline.

Before you report what you notice, encourage the client to share what they see and how they feel as they take in the complexity and totality of the map. This is often the first time they have seen the whole 'picture' in this way. Their reaction is important data in itself.

Ask them to check if they have a sense of completeness or if something is missing. If this is the case, they might not be able to 'put their finger on it' in the moment. It will often emerge to the surface later, in which case they can add it in afterwards.

Once you have provided space for this reflection, look for and harvest the themes and repeating patterns, together.

This gathering and acknowledging of history can be spread over several sessions – it is a fundamental part of the process and should not be rushed.

Recommended exercise – reconnect with your roots

When you have distilled the key themes and repeating patterns from the history map, it can be very helpful to initiate the following strengthening and resourcing exercise. This can be used as a powerful pause and reflection point before moving on to the next phase.

In this exercise, it is recommended to fully use the floor space and get the client to move into the relevant spaces identified below. It is also possible to do this as a desktop exercise with post-it notes, depending on the comfort level of the client and whether the session is virtual or in person.

Minimum materials are needed for this session – paper markers (A4) or post-it notes.

Using A4 pieces of paper (or post-it notes), create markers entitled as follows:

ENTITLE MARKERS AS FOLLOWS	GUIDING NOTES
ME	A marker to represent the client so that when they step back to review the architecture of what is set up – they can see where they are as part of it
MY HERITAGE X 2	One marker to represent paternal line & one marker to represent maternal line
DIRECT FAMILY	One marker to represent their direct family set up (i.e. wife/husband/partner and children, where relevant)
PURPOSE	This relates to whole life purpose (this can be included even if this is not yet clear to them)
MY EMERGING FUTURE	What life wants from me – what's calling me? (i.e. beyond the current plan or ego that may be driving for something specific)
WORK EXPERIENCE	One marker for each organisation
SKILLS & TRAINING	One marker to represent all of this is sufficient unless the client feels it's important to have emphasis on something specific
CORE VALUES	A marker for each of these; if there are more than five – get them to prioritise
MENTORS, GUIDES & TEACHERS	One marker to represent these as a group
TODAY'S DATE	The current year

The process

Timelines – Using the physical space in the room, ask the client to decide for themselves which end of the room depicts their past, and which end represents the future for them. Once established, ask them to identify the area on that timeline that represents today. When chosen, ask them to place the markers for 'My Emerging Future' and 'Today' on the floor, to create a timeline.

Self and family – Ask the client to place the marker for themselves, their direct family and the two markers for the paternal and maternal ancestors in their family (just one marker for each side of the family). Let the client figure out where each of these are – invite them to trust their intuition and place them accordingly.

Taking your place – This step is about being aware and honouring this heritage and ensuring they are in their right place and the 'right size' in the sequence of time, with their ancestors 'at their back'.

Invite the client to take their place on the timeline by standing on the marker that represents them. Give them time to really arrive there and invite them to quieten down any verbal chatter so that they can really start to notice their physical sensations and energy. Standing with the ancestors behind them can feel very resourcing and often creates a grounding effect, but everyone is different. Stay free of expectations – let them notice how it is for them.

When they have settled and if they are comfortable to share, ask them how it is, with their ancestors 'at their back' and their direct family fully present.

Ask them to turn around and face their ancestors for a moment and offer them a sentence to hold quietly or say out loud, as they look back at their ancestors.

"Without you, none of this would be possible. Because of you and all that you gave, I am here."

It can sometimes happen that individuals will resist acknowledging this reality and if so, offer them a slightly adjusted sentence, as follows:

"I hate to admit it, but without you, none of this would be possible and because of you and all that you gave, I am here."

Purpose and core values – Ask the client where they want the markers for purpose and core values, and add these to the timeline for them. Purpose is likely to be in front of them (so they can see it) and values are typically placed close to the client as well and they may wish to stand on these. Once again, invite them to trust their intuition in terms of where they want each of these markers to be placed relative to where they are on the timeline.

If you are working face to face, you can place these on behalf of the client whilst they remain on their own marker. If this is the case, ensure to place each of the relevant markers where the client wants them as opposed to where you believe they should be.

Work experience, skills and training – Finally, invite the client to direct you to the location for the rest of the markers and add these to complete the timeline. These final markers represent resources.

Pause to take it all in – When placed, invite the client to look all around and to take a few minutes to take it all in.

Finally, let them fully acknowledge how this is for them – to have their entire heritage behind them and all of their family and resources around them, with their future trajectory on the horizon.

Some clients may like to verbalise it; they may find it helpful for you to capture the essence of their words (and share it later as a reminder). Some will relish a photo of the timeline and finally, others will prefer to take it all in, in silence, so all the value is internalised. There is no need to rush this final element – it's a few minutes of high value!

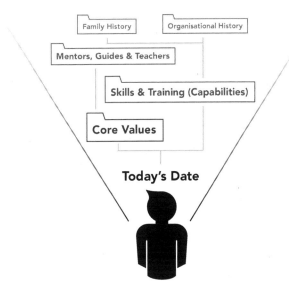

Acknowledging the whole person and both systems

As part of his successful career in large-scale global organisations, Archie had travelled extensively gathering a multitude of experience along the way.

He had secured a series of successive promotions over the past ten years, but when we started working together, he had just been declined a significant promotion. This was unfamiliar territory for Archie.

Feedback from the recruitment process was that he was not fully prepared and this came across as arrogance. The story was that he approached the recruitment process like the job was already his. He worked in an organisation that was highly networked and the story people had about you travelled quickly. Your leadership brand mattered.

Archie was part of the leadership for the sales division, which was seen as the 'engine room' of the organisation, and he had an exceptionally good relationship with his boss.

As part of the coaching journey, we started by understanding his history, by gathering information on the 'history map'. As Archie was very open to the process, we started mapping his personal history and then moved across to complete the picture with his organisational experience.

By going through his personal history, we very quickly identified that he had a need to be seen and where this need was coming from. He had one sibling who was seen as the shining light in the family. Archie, as a consequence, felt like he was constantly in their shadow and so he had learned, from a young age, how to compensate. He found ways to move himself into the spotlight in order to get the attention he craved. This unconscious pattern was showing up in the organisational setting and was interpreted as ego and arrogance.

We also talked through the highs, lows and significant moments of his organisational history. By unpacking some of his difficult experiences in the organisational timeline, it became very apparent where some of his core values were birthed.

When reviewing the personal development journey with someone, a really helpful phrase to keep in mind here is: "Our voids become our values". Those unmet needs often inform our core values, and this was certainly the case with Archie.

When the history mapping was complete, I invited him to stand in his history map and look back at where he had come from. We took some time to acknowledge his journey, the good, the challenging and all the learnings in between.

We particularly acknowledged the parallels between the patterns of the personal and organisational systems. By doing so, we honoured that all of his history had a place. It had made him who he was and was stronger for it.

Before identifying which of these patterns he wanted to carry with him versus which he needed to 'put down', we took in feedback from his stakeholders. We'll pick up with Archie again in the next chapter.

PERCOLATIONS...

After mapping your own history, here's some questions to support you:

1. What needs to be honoured?

2. What do you want to bring with you?

3. What patterns might you have been/be susceptible to?

4. What inner work is required in order that you can respectfully leave this behind you?

CHAPTER SEVEN

ACKNOWLEDGE CURRENT REALITY

Having understood and respectfully acknowledged where the client has come from and all of the challenges along that path, you also need to acknowledge the reality of where the coaching journey begins. Within this early phase, it's vital that you take into consideration multiple perspectives so that you can ensure you don't get pulled into the same blind spots as the client.

This phase is about gathering an understanding of what's going well, where the client is adding value, where things might have got stuck, information on any challenges or difficult relationships and the perspective on their potential.

With this in mind, it is recommended that 360-degree feedback is gathered, i.e. views are collected from those working around the client, which would include but are not limited to their:

1. Line Manager

2. Peers

3. Direct Reports

Depending on the seniority of the individual, I would also recommend connecting with the second line manager and an appropriate person within the HR team, who is likely to be aware of any relevant succession planning information.

To provide insights around the consistency of their behaviour, and to check if it's conditional on the environment, I would occasionally also include a contribution from someone or a few individuals outside of the organisation who know the client well. This is especially helpful if the client has an externally-facing role.

This could be someone from a previous organisation (especially relevant if the client has worked elsewhere for a long period of time), an external mentor, their life partner or a relevant client or customer.

From the combination of perspectives above, you will harvest a robust sense of what they are consistently doing that adds value, if/how they might be diluting value and what needs attention with regard to their leadership brand as you stand alongside them on the 'starting grid'.

There are a variety of 360-degree feedback tools that you can utilise and your choice may come down to what you are most comfortable with. I would strongly recommend a methodology that will give you a mix of quantitative and qualitative information.

My preference is to utilise a conversational approach, i.e. speaking directly with each stakeholder. These calls generally take approximately forty minutes. In this relatively short period of time, it gives you the valuable opportunity as themes start to emerge, to probe and dig deeper. It is important to get beyond the generalisations and surface-level symptoms that are offered.

In this setting, you can start to establish an understanding of the context. You need to get underneath the symptoms, listen out for the repeating patterns, and start the critical task of surfacing the root cause. In addition, it gives you the opportunity to gather valuable specifics and rich examples of the 'issues' that are being highlighted. This direct conversation also provides the opportunity to gently encourage those stakeholders to look beyond their current narrative/story.

In my experience, the client is much more attuned to hearing the feedback when there are specific examples that bring the themes from their stakeholders to life. It helps them to make sense of the feedback and take it seriously.

Detailed below is the recommended approach for conversational 360 feedback. This combination of questions will help you get to the core elements of leadership that are vital to creating and maintaining a healthy system as referenced in chapter 2.

Suggested questions for conversational 360 feedback.

THE ORDERING FORCES AND PRINCIPLES THAT ENABLE RELATIONSHIPS AND A HEALTHY ECOSYSTEM				
	CONTRIBUTION	MUTUAL EXCHANGE	PLACE	BELONGING
GOING WELL	1.What do they do that adds value to others/ the function/the wider system? *Gather specifics & examples	3.To what degree do they establish and facilitate a balance of giving and taking? 1/10 *Gather specifics & examples	5.To what degree do they take their 'full place' in the team/function/business? (1/10) *Gather specifics & examples 8.To what degree do they set up their team/function/ business to take its full place in the wider system? (1/10) *Gather specifics & examples	8.To what extent do they enable and nurture a sense of belonging within their team/ function/ business (1/10)?
POTENTIAL AREAS OF FOCUS	2.What do they do that dilutes value (albeit unconsciously) to others/the function/the wider system? *Gather specifics & examples	4.What needs attention in relation to their stakeholder relationships – i.e. what needs to happen/be different in order to get them closer to a score of 10?	6.When might they take more than their right and full place in the system (i.e. they are too big) OR where/when might they not fully step into their right and full place (playing small)? *Gather specifics & examples 7.What do you notice as the repeating pattern when either of the above scenarios happen? *Gather specifics & examples	9.What needs attention in regard to people feeling like they belong within this individual's area of responsibility? *Gather specific suggestions

BROADER AREAS OF LEADERSHIP	THE ORDERING FORCES AND PRINCIPLES THAT ENABLE RELATIONSHIPS AND A HEALTHY ECOSYSTEM
	10. PURPOSE: a. To what extent is the sense of purpose that has been created for the part of the business this person is responsible for, clear and understood? (Score 1/10)? b. To what degree is this purpose being realised (1/10)? c. What needs attention? *Gather specifics and examples* 11. LEADERSHIP BRAND a. If you could sum this individual up in a few words, what would those words be? b. If we were speaking again in circa 12 months, how would you love to be describing this individual (in a few words)? 12. VITALITY & POTENTIAL FOR MOVEMENT To what extent do you sense a level of vitality and potential for forwards momentum in the system that this person is responsible for? (10 = high level of vitality & momentum and 1 = the system is stuck/toxic) 13. SUCCESS CRITERA If this coaching assignment was deemed to be a huge success, from your perspective.... a. What would you see/hear/experience that is different (for you/the team/the wider business)? b. What impact would this have (on you/the team/the wider business)? *Gather specifics and examples* c. How will you know when this has happened (indicators/success criteria)?

Having gathered the stakeholder feedback, it is recommended that you distil this into a user-friendly format that supports your debriefing conversation so that the client can share this with their line manager in due course.

Creating sufficient space and time for talking through the feedback with the client and encouraging subsequent reflection is critical. I tend to set aside a minimum of two hours with the individual for the debrief and then give them a minimum of a week to reflect before drawing out the key themes that are worthy of focused attention.

Equally important is that their line manager is involved at this stage of the process. When the client has had sufficient time to reflect, they are encouraged to follow up with their line manager, and together, conclude on a maximum of three priority focus areas. This involves agreeing the success criteria at a sufficient level of detail so that all three of us are clear and aligned with what great progress looks like.

Equipped with these priority focus areas and success criteria, you are in a position to support the client in identifying the patterns that are relevant. Some of these will be enabling their success and can therefore be leveraged and carried forward. Some of the active patterns, however, may be limiting.

When you have this level of clarity you are ready to help the client move to the next step, releasing limiting patterns.

Where are the patterns showing up?

"Something has to change – I can't withstand this tension for much longer", were the words from an exhausted CFO.

Derek was an experienced chief financial officer (CFO), with more than ten years of service within a publicly listed company. He had just been moved to a new role in one of the businesses within the group.

Derek was asked to take up the CFO role to support a relatively new CEO as part of his longer-term career trajectory within the group.

Derek and his CEO were joining a fairly well-established executive team and a business that was facing significant challenges within a highly competitive sector.

Derek had been in his new role for six months when we met. As part of the coaching process, 360 feedback was gathered, so that Derek could be certain of where he was on 'the starting grid', with his CEO and his executive team peers.

There was very positive feedback about Derek's capabilities and the value he could add to the division, however it became apparent that he had not yet settled into the team. In fact, his peers felt he was more loyal to the wider business rather than to the division.

The CEO really needed to sense that he was alongside him as a strong business partner and confidant. The feedback from the CEO, however, was that Derek seemed to be holding himself as quite separate and was often taking the lead in strategic initiatives without proactively consulting him. It did not yet feel like a trusted partnership.

The information gathered at this early stage suggested Derek clearly had the capabilities and the experience that was required. From a systemic perspective, however, there were potential issues around his sense of place and the flow of leadership (these essential ingredients of a healthy system are referenced in Chapter 2).

The distinction between his place and that of the CEO was blurred and there was some fuzziness around what got escalated to the CEO desk versus what was taken care of by the CFO.

We'll come back to Derek in chapter 12 to talk more about these potentially limiting patterns and how we worked with them.

Another client example of needing to look beyond the symptoms when gathering 360 feedback was with Archie, who we met in the previous chapter.

Archie was a highly effective and successful specialist working in a global role, within a large, complex and highly-networked FMCG organisation. Within this organisation, your leadership brand mattered.

He had been consistently successful in a series of promotions throughout his career leading up to and within the current organisation. He had recently put himself forward for a significant promotion and for the first time in his career, this progression was declined.

He felt like he had hit a 'ceiling' and had received feedback that there was a perception in the business that he had become too confident and for some, was perceived as needing to 'be in the spotlight'.

The 360 feedback demonstrated exceptionally strong feedback from his line manager but to the point where his peers felt excluded and lacked confidence in his ability to be a neutral sounding board.

His core strength in building relationships was highlighted and there was no question that he had the experience and capabilities for further progression, but there were some questions about his leadership brand.

The insights from the history mapping were confirmed by the 360 feedback, in that he seemed to have a need to be 'front and centre' of significant initiatives. Within the work context, he needed to be seen to be in the lead. The perception was that he appeared to be leading with a strong sense of ego.

With regard to the leadership of the team, he had recruited a strong, capable and highly-respected team. Archie had done a superb job of getting the right team and structure in place. The requests coming through from his team were about needing more time with him, and the more experienced members of the team wanted to feel further empowered.

From a systemic perspective, the repeating pattern in his personal system was the need to be seen and acknowledged – this unmet need was showing up in the organisational context. With regard to his role, the areas that needed attention were mostly about place and purpose.

He was choosing to stand beside his boss as a trusted partner but excluding the part of his role as an objective thought partner for his peers. In an organisation that was going through significant and complex change, the team's collective capability and confidence to deliver would be a critical contributor to the realisation of the vision.

We'll come back to how we helped Archie release his limiting patterns and significantly transform his leadership brand, within chapter 12.

CHAPTER EIGHT

RELEASE LIMITING PATTERNS

The approach of the more classic coaching methodologies is to acknowledge the starting point and identify where the individual wants to shift to. This could be about adopting a set of new behaviours or more mid/longer term, about attaining their career ambitions.

Having understood the start line and the expected 'finish line', the job at hand for the coach is to help the individual chart a course on how to move towards this desired end point. This process is coherent and entirely logical – and to be perfectly honest, was deployed consistently in my early years of coaching both as an internal coach and subsequently, as an external coach.

However, what I witnessed in my own development and in that of my clients, was that the limiting patterns that had been embedded for some time, and operated unconsciously, just resurfaced later, perhaps in another form or in another context.

The root cause had not been identified and the positive intention or systemic function of these patterns was therefore never fully acknowledged. The consequence of this was that the entanglement remained and just continued to show up like a boomerang that kept coming back!

When you have gathered the stakeholder feedback, you are aiming to identify the individual's repeating patterns, discern which serve them in their current context and which are no longer enabling their wellbeing, their performance or their highest potential.

Work at the pace and depth your client is ready for

Your role as coach is to stand alongside your client and to support them in zooming back. From there, it is about unpacking these patterns and discerning what the individual is ready to work on. It is important to work at a pace and a depth the client is ready for.

It is often the case that you will work with each layer of complexity as the individual becomes more comfortable with the approach and the trust is built between you.

Go slow now, in order to create the trust and safety to go faster later

---

Work within your capabilities

Be careful not to go too deep too quickly, and be super conscious of your own limitations in terms of capability. Only open up what you feel comfortable and capable of working with.

We will cover the most prevalent limiting patterns mentioned earlier, in terms of how they may be showing up in the organisational context.

We will not cover how you would explicitly and directly delve into and start working with the patterns that are coming from the personal system (this requires more extensive training). Instead, we will demonstrate how you can help the client to separate them from coming up in the organisational setting through the context overlay intervention detailed below.

Resources to help you get to the root cause

For sustainable breakthroughs, it is critical to help the individual zoom back to understand where these patterns may be coming from and for what purpose, i.e. get to the root cause.

There are a range of resources that can help with this:

- The history 'map' is your starting point, as recommended in Chapter 6.

- The fundamental principles of a healthy system (the 3 x Os), referenced in Chapter 1, provide a lens to look through.

- Percolation questions from Chapter 2 help you dig deeper.

Finally, in your reflections on the systemic function of the repeating patterns, the following questions may be of further benefit:

- What is the system trying to communicate through this pattern?

- What could be the very good reason for this?

- What is this limiting pattern a solution for?

- What is the unmet need of the wider system?

- Which of the fundamental principles have been breached, distorted or disrupted?

Who are you working with?

Bear in mind that there are a variety of levels that clients' patterns could be operating at. By reviewing the 'history map', you can determine the kind of intervention that might be required.

If you are working with an individual, then you are reviewing their personal system (family dynamics) and their career journey to date. As per the note above, if you do not feel equipped to work with the content that surfaces from the personal system, gather the themes and information on the patterns from this part of the history map but stop short of opening things up too much.

If the individual leader is responsible for a business, then it would be entirely appropriate to review the organisational history and the patterns therein, as is suggested below.

If you are working with a group, e.g. a leadership team or the whole organisation, then you need to review the history of the organisation as a whole system, including how it was founded and where it sits in relation to the ecosystem.

The scope of your coaching assignment

If you are dealing with a distortion of the ordering principles that has just started in the current context, i.e. it is happening in the here and now, but has not been a recurring issue, then the entanglements are likely to be closer to the surface, and therefore more accessible to work with.

If, however, this pattern has been repeating for some time, then you probably need to address a distortion of the ordering principles a bit further back in time. This will require delving further back on the 'history map' to discern when this distortion or disruption commenced and deal with it at the root cause.

Bearing in mind the visual of how patterns form from Chapter 3, the overall intention is to get beyond the symptoms and travel back to the source event and root cause.

When we can get back to the root cause of any pattern and acknowledge what it was trying to do for the system, we have a chance of releasing the pattern and freeing up the client for sustained forward momentum.

Once again, caution is encouraged here. Go at the pace the individual is ready for and only work on that which you feel comfortable and confident with.

The overarching process

When you are working with any of the patterns, the overall process flow is the same:

1. Honour history

2. Acknowledge what is (the source event, the impact and the limiting pattern)

3. Release the limiting pattern (making sure to harvest the gifts before the pattern is released)

The methodology

Shifting repeating patterns at their root cause is done so through two key types of intervention:

- The use of specific sentences that acknowledge the root cause and its impact

- Through movement – this can be literal movement of the individual via markers used to represent elements of the system or via an inner movement within the client triggered through conversation

The methodology for facilitating these movements follows the same four-step sequence, as follows:

1. Capture and review history on a timeline ('history map') to identify the repeating patterns as per Chapter 6.

2. Create a multidimensional map of the system today. This is the **AS IS POSITION** i.e. how things are right now and not how the individual would like it to be. This map can be created using post-it notes, A4 paper or physical objects.

3. Utilise specific sentence structures to pinpoint the entanglement and release the limiting patterns, ensuring the gifts (learnings, insights, experience gathered) are explicitly harvested.

4. Experiment through adjusting the map, to find a construct that allows the system to settle, regain vitality and with the freedom to move.

It is important not to rush the process. It needs space and time

It is important not to rush any of the stages above. Whilst they are relatively straightforward, they are not simple. This process is often asking the individual to work at an unconscious level which requires a level of spaciousness.

The process facilitates profound movements within the client and in their relationship to the issue/system but aren't immediately obvious or visible straightaway.

Working with each of the patterns

The rest of this chapter is dedicated to giving you an overview of the typical interventions that will be appropriate for each of those prevalent patterns mentioned earlier.

It is important to emphasise that each client scenario will be unique and there might be a combination of limiting patterns activated simultaneously. Work with each one separately.

Context overlay

Where two contexts have been collapsed together

This is one of the more prevalent dynamics that you are likely to come across and is therefore the recommended priority intervention process to have in your toolkit.

This is where two different contexts have been collapsed together. They could encompass a collapsing of two separate organisational issues but could also entail the personal dimension being laid on top of the organisational aspect.

The symptom to look out for is a significantly higher level of emotional charge that would be reasonable to expect for the organisational issue in hand.

The essence of the intervention is to help the client see that this collapse has taken place and to separate these two contexts.

If the personal dimension is laid over the organisational, it's important to note that you don't have to work with this personal aspect. It is often enough to help the client register the collapse has taken place and then 'move it' to one side.

This will create the space for the client to focus on the organisational dimension at hand and then choose how, when, and with whom, they want to look at the personal aspect (if at all).

Recommended process

Step 1

Create a new marker to represent the 'other context' – this can be another post-it note, an A4 piece of paper or an object, chosen by the client.

Step 2

Ask the client to bring the new marker into the multidimensional map.

Step 3

Having specified what the marker represents at a conceptual level, e.g. the other context that is here, ask the client where it belongs in the 'As is' map.

It is vitally important to emphasise that you do *not* need to know what the additional context is, and is especially important in the instance that the additional layer is from the personal dimension. It is only important that it is separated and that the client is able to determine where a 'safe place' would be from their point of view.

Step 4

Experimenting with the distance of this marker. The further away from the client it is, the better. More distance normally provokes more relaxation and settling, which is what you are aiming for.

As you leave the marker for this 'other context' in its position (as far away from the client as is needed), introduce the sentence below (you may need to repeat it a few times):

"This other context is here – it is safe and it is separate. You can look at it whenever you are ready and until then, it is held in a safe place."

When the client has become less emotionally charged, you can help the client turn their attention back to what needs their energy and focus.

Identification

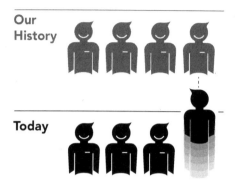

This is where individuals, roles, functions or divisions are identified with a particular person, function or unresolved issue that has been excluded.

The current incumbents are not fully available in the here and now. Part of them is caught up in a dynamic or limiting pattern that is reminiscent of something or someone that is missing. You will normally find the clues in the history map of the organisation.

The consequence of this pattern is that the individual cannot operate at their optimum and will often be experiencing the sensations of the excluded part. The dynamic of identification is the system's way of sacrificing the individual dimension in service of the whole. It is using this process to alert the current incumbents/ leaders that something important needs attention.

The essence of the intervention is to free up the individual (this can be one person, but also a function or a division) from the experience of unconsciously adopting the characteristics and experiencing the sensations of the element which is missing.

It's about enabling the missing element to be remembered and fully included in the history.

Recommended process

Step 1 – Reintroduce what has been excluded

As a first step in resolving this dynamic, it can be supremely helpful to introduce something (a marker or an object) to represent the excluded entity and place it on the physical map that has been created.

Step 2 – Get into contact with the excluded part and acknowledge it

By including it, acknowledging it and remembering it explicitly, individuals within the system no longer have to unconsciously expend energy in 'holding and remembering it' on behalf of the wider system. It is included again.

Step 3 – Sentence work

It can be helpful to invite the client (or the person/part that was identified) to 'connect with' (look at) the excluded entity and offer the client some sentences.

Invite them to vocalise whichever sentences feel most resonant from the list below, and to share these sentences with the excluded entity.

These sentences can be said inwardly or externalised, depending on the preference of the individual.

"I was remembering you unconsciously – now I will remember you consciously."

If the excluded entity had made a significant contribution to the business, then a relevant additional sentence might be: *"We won't forget you."*

Upon completion of the sentence work, check in with the client – take note of what they say and what you notice about them.

Distortions of place

Being pulled out of your right place

- Triangulation (pulled one level up – to the same level as your boss)

- Parentification (pulled two levels up – to the level above your boss)

When there is a void at the levels above, individuals can be unconsciously recruited to fill the vacuum one or two levels up.

Whilst this will have been done with good intention and most likely to be helpful, it is not necessarily a sustainable or healthy position for the individual. They end up carrying responsibility that is not theirs to carry, vacating their right place in the system and can end up feeling like they don't belong anywhere.

This can be the territory for exhaustion and burnout.

The essence of the interventions for both dynamics of distortion of place is about right-sizing the individuals who are triangulated or parentified.

It's about helping them realise they have stepped up/been pulled up and finding their way back to their right place and right size. This enables them to secure a more sustainable sense of belonging again.

Recommended process

The process for both of these distortions of place is the same. For simplicity, the process below outlines how this works for the pattern of triangulation.

The client may prefer to use objects rather than pieces of paper as this can often help the scenario and the sentence work feel more authentic. This will, of course, be partly informed by the environment in which the coaching is taking place.

Step 1

Set up markers/objects for the person who is triangulated AND the other individuals who are relevant in this scenario.

For example, if they were triangulated with their line manager, set up markers for the client, the line manager and another marker to represent the client's peers.

Step 2

Invite the individual to set up the relevant markers/objects in the space available.

Ask them to stand on their own marker and get into contact (look at) the marker/object for the line manager.

Step 3

Invite them to explicitly acknowledge the specific gifts/insights/learnings they have gathered from stepping up to the next level.

Step 4

Offer them the following sentences and let them experiment until such time as they feel congruent:

"I took your place in the system and it has weakened both of us."

"I'm sorry I didn't see your strength."

"I have gained many gifts from occupying this place. I will treasure them and build upon them. The rest, I leave with you."

"You are my manager, I am your direct report."

"You are our senior leader, I am just a member of the team."

If there is some resistance to these, try adding a prefix, as follows:

"I hate to admit it, but you are my manager and I am your direct report."

It may be necessary for a few iterations of these sentences, before they really land with the individual. This will especially be the case if they have been occupying that 'bigger place' for some time.

Step 5

Once the sentences work and harvesting of the gifts is complete, encourage the client to experiment with finding their right place relative to their seniors and peers.

Finally, as is the case with all of the other interventions, check how your client is before signing off the session. Give them some space to reflect and decompress. They have probably been holding this tension for some time. It can be an emotional experience!

Polarisation

Caught between two extremes – occupying one end of the spectrum and disowning the other.

There's a part that we feel comfortable with. We find the other dimension repulsive and have a tendency to feel bigger or better than it. The reality however, is that both parts exist and we actually also embody this 'other part' without realising it. This dynamic is outside of our conscious awareness.

This pattern is calling attention to the fact that both parts want to come together and reconcile a split that has happened further back in time.

The essence of the intervention is to free up the individual from holding (and being affected by) the polarity, and to reintroduce the context within which the original split happened. This has the added benefit of also right-sizing the client.

Recommended process

Step 1

Ask the client to create two markers (or objects) to represent each end of the polarity that they are pulled between.

It is ideal to place the markers on the floor so that the physical space can be utilised, however, if you are working virtually, post-it notes on the desk can also work.

Step 2

Invite the client to connect with (or stand upon) the markers at each end of the polarity. Ask them to register and share what they notice each time.

In order to release the limiting patterns, it's helpful in the first instance to really connect with it and acknowledge its presence and impact.

Step 3

When they have had enough time to gather some insight on each dimension of the polarity, ask them to introduce a third marker/object into the space.

Make them aware that this element represents the bigger context (which may be further back in time) within which both of these extremes absolutely belong and, in fact, co-exist.

Ask the client to shift to a position when they can see this bigger context, and that the polarity belongs in this context. This will normally mean that they need to create some distance between themselves and the other three markers – this movement of separation is what you are looking for.

Step 4

Give them a few moments to internalise this new map and give them some time to capture and share a sense of the gifts (insights, learnings, new/enhanced capabilities) they have gathered as a result of holding the tension of these two polarities.

Summary

Just to recap, once you have surfaced the tension, the limiting patterns and uncovered the root cause, the process has three key stages:

1. Honour history

2. Acknowledge what is (the source event, the impact and the limiting pattern)

3. Release the limiting pattern (making sure to harvest the gifts before the pattern is released)

The systemic process is simple, precise and profound. It is a catalyst for immense settling and movement.

It is critical that space and time are created for the incubation period and reflection, not least because most of the movement is happening at an unconscious level.

I would strongly recommend checking in with individuals twenty-four/forty-eight hours after a session, when the rational sense-making element will be kicking in.

I often use the phrase: "Your body knows, and your head will catch up."

'Your body knows, your head will catch up'

CHAPTER NINE

NURTURE SYSTEMIC AWARENESS

LOOKING BEYOND

I'm learning…

It is not all about now, or me, or you

I'm learning…

To look further

To look behind

To look beneath

I'm learning…

I'm learning…

To widen my gaze

To soften my eyes

To listen to my gut

To trust that inner voice

To pause before I leap

I'm learning…

I'm learning…

To ask

What's the lesson?

Why this?

Why now?

I'm learning…

I'm learning…

To look for the pattern

The deeper reason

To find its roots

And set it free

I'm learning…

I'm learning…

When it can all be seen

Released and settled

We are free

To move

And that's worth learning…

Your role

In the first instance, your role is to build your client's self-awareness and enable them to fully take their place in their leadership role.

This starts with supporting them to do their own 'work' and taking time to understand their own history (personal and professional) as described in chapter 7. This will ensure they become more aware of their own patterns, where they come from and what triggers them.

The reality is, you are building the self-awareness within the client throughout the coaching process. Over time, they will be more able to decipher what is going on for themselves, the parts of the system they influence and pick up the dynamics in the wider system.

Your ultimate aim is to help them become more self-sufficient by awakening their systemic intelligence and equipping them to constructively navigate the various complexities they will encounter. This includes building their ability to bring patterns and dynamics to the surface quickly, so that they can ensure the root cause can be uncovered, acknowledged and understood.

> Enabling the individual to develop their systemic intelligence is not a one-off piece of work

Enabling the individual to develop their systemic capabilities isn't a one-off piece of work or a download from coach to client. Whilst it is recommended that you create a point of emphasis at this stage in the coaching journey, it is not intended that this is the only moment where the learning is happening.

Nurturing this intelligence within the client is something that needs to happen the whole way through the coaching journey but it is helpful to punctuate the coaching process with a spotlight on the 'how' of this approach at various stages.

This helps to ensure the learnings are being embedded and that they have the tools they need as they become more self-sufficient over time.

Leveraging multiple intelligence systems

Part of the learning process is to build and trust our various internal intelligence systems. Within business, it is not unusual for logic and rational thinking to be the primary vehicle for gathering understanding of what is going on.

The brain in our head is the primary intelligence toolkit that is developed and emphasised within the schooling system. Sadly, other equally powerful intelligences are at best latent and at worst, actively dismissed.

The heart has its own complex nervous system and communication between the brain and the heart takes the form of a dynamic and ongoing two-way dialogue. Communication happens in four major ways: neurologically, biochemically, biophysically and energetically. Put more simply, messages sent from the heart to the brain are multidimensional and can ultimately affect performance.

The third intelligence system is your gut. We often hear the phrase "listen to your gut instinct" and the advice here is to take that information very seriously. Scientists sometimes call this brain the second brain. It is made up of two thin layers of more than 100 million nerve cells which have the capacity to carry extensive information back to the main brain – in our head. [4]

Decision-making is traditionally viewed as a rational process whereby logical reasoning calculates the best way to achieve the goal. More recent developments in science, however, have found that this combination of the neural systems in the head, heart and gut appear to be involved in higher-order human functioning and decision-making.

Solutions to technical problems lie in the head and solving them requires intellect and logic. Solutions to complex, adaptive problems however, lie in the gut and in the heart.

Leading complex change relies on being able to bring people with it, and is often asking people to change their beliefs, habits and ways of working. Employees will more often respond emotionally and from their gut in these situations, so being able to connect with and tap into this well of intelligence is key.

As the organisational context will only continue to increase in complexity, leaders who can leverage a range of intelligences and trust their gut and intuition are required.

The suggestion in the realm of systemic work is that these intelligences are potentially picking up the signals of the wider system and rather than dismiss them, take these signals seriously as another form of data, to be explored alongside the rational information that is offered.

In summary, a lot of information is passing between us through these complex intelligence systems and bypassing the rational thought process. Developing the ability to listen to the signals, nuances and undercurrent is a critical skill in a context of ever-increasing levels of complexity.

Essential skills

It is important to develop your client's ability to really listen. It's a quality of listening that is sensitive to any undercurrent, able to identify symptoms and join together information on the repeating patterns.

In addition to listening to the signals of the wider system, there are a variety of skills that are fundamental to building capability to work with the insights.

These include the ability and willingness to slow down, zoom back and develop a wide lens. Equally important is patience, suspending any judgment and the ability to hold off on the potential rush into sense-making too soon.

It's important to stay open-minded, curious and judgment-free – at least for a bit longer than might be the case otherwise.

Client example

"I don't want to be another casualty of this system," declared Jemma, after another frustrating exchange with her functional line manager.

We met Jemma earlier, in Chapter 3. She had become established in her organisation and her function was outperforming expectations.

However, she had a challenging relationship with her functional line manager which was not logical. They had previously been peers and had a good relationship. This changed when her peer was promoted to the seat of the role of global head of HR, and her functional line manager.

Because we had already done a lot of work within a previous systemic coaching journey, Jemma had a good level of self- and systemic awareness so she was alert to the potential that this dysfunctional relationship might have nothing to do with her or the specific individual.

When we delved deeper as part of the work on the history of her role, it became clear that this dysfunction had previously been active when her predecessor was in the 'role' and specifically between her role and the role of the functional line manager. This dynamic was pertinent to the roles rather than the people and had been in action and repeating for some time.

Her predecessor had been exited, as had the incumbent before that. There were incidents that had happened previously that had not been acknowledged and the system was ejecting each person who took this role, until this phenomenon could get the attention it deserved. The seat needed to be unburdened in order for anyone to settle in the job.

This dysfunction was embedded within the roles and was not about the individuals. In another situation, and without this systemic awareness, it would have been very easy for Jemma to assume this was all about her, and for the dynamics to escalate such that the functional line manager would have no option but to decide to exit Jemma as had happened with her two predecessors.

Instead, through a systemic coaching session dedicated to working through this scenario, Jemma was able to step outside the dynamic and facilitate a different conversation.

Ultimately the wider system was restructured and the roles within this global function were reshaped, thereby enabling Jemma to take her full place and continue to drive the exceptional results through her team.

Jemma wasn't able to fully influence the whole system – it wasn't her place to do so, but she was able to untangle herself from this dysfunctional exchange. Through acknowledging the difficulty and complexity that her functional line manager was also unconsciously steeped within, Jemma was able to be empathic and stay in respectful mode.

She was able to be more patient and understand why the exceptional results from her team could not be fully seen, no matter how frustrating. And finally, she could be more intentional and constructive about how she wanted to show up from a leadership standpoint.

This patience and intentionality won through – after the business was reshaped, she was promoted to take on responsibility for the global function. She did not have to be another casualty of the ejector seat dynamic!

Summary

In summary, this phase is about putting a focus on awakening and nurturing systemic awareness. There is an emphasis within this phase but will continually happen throughout the coaching process.

Your ultimate aim is to develop your client's systemic awareness and capabilities so that in time, they become more self-sufficient and are alert to, and able to constructively work with, systemic patterns.

CHAPTER TEN

ENGAGE WITH THE UPCOMING FUTURE

It's not unusual for leaders to have a sense of what they want to move towards. This can be fuelled by a strong ego and high self-esteem. It can be informed by their upbringing, their education, their commitments to and the expectations from others. This combination of factors can create an impetus and drive to progress.

It can, however, bring with it an overriding essence of the future that is dictated by what they should do or should be striving for rather than listening to what is innately calling them.

This can materialise into an element of disillusionment and the individual can end up feeling that they are almost following a path that isn't wholly theirs. This may, in fact, be the trigger to initiate the coaching process.

We call this phenomenon of having a strong sense of direction and a future that is all mapped out, the planned future. It's a known quantity and they are planning to make it happen for themselves. They know what they want to do with their life and when this is the case, the client may be simply seeking to get your help, guidance and support to make this happen.

From a systemic perspective, there is a second dimension to the future which is more about opening up to the possibility that rather than us driving towards the future (with a plan), the future is coming towards us and will happen whether we have a plan or not.

This essence of the upcoming future can be applied across various dimensions, i.e. the individual, team/function as well as the whole business.

Connecting with this evolutionary force can be a very helpful stage in the coaching journey. It can support sense-checking of any previous 'planned future' as well as creating space for new possibilities to enter the horizon. This is particularly relevant when someone is coming to the close of their particular assignment or has been in a role for a reasonable period of time and is getting itchy feet as they start to prepare for their next move.

If the client is early into their role, this step of engaging with the upcoming future may be more applicable to the wider system. This could be especially relevant if their business is a challenge. This insight can help inform what needs to be on the radar from an organisational standpoint and therefore, inform the nature of leadership that will be required.

There are a variety of ways in which you can work with this evolutionary force. You can wholly rely on more of a sensing approach that is free of structure. This can be both valuable and relevant when the client is able to connect with all of their intelligences as mentioned in Chapter 9. There are also degrees of structure that can be incorporated based on preferred ways of working.

Semi-structured approach

Some individuals might prefer a more tangible and concrete approach. In this scenario, it is recommended that you adopt a semi-structured approach to connect with the upcoming future.

An example of doing this would be by getting them back on to their timeline (created in Chapter 6). When they have settled there, invite them to energetically connect with the upcoming future on that timeline. Check what they notice and harvest the insights from that position.

Structured approach

The exercise below is a recommended structured approach that creates a helpful frame and a very safe container for the client. This is the approach we mentioned in Chapter 2, with Laura, who was reviewing career options.

Mapping options exercise

At a headline level, you are effectively creating a 2 x 2 matrix within which the client will place their options.

If you are working face to face, then you can optimise the opportunity of the space. If you are working virtually, you can still ask the individual to utilise their own space whilst you guide and support them through the process via your preferred virtual platform.

If on the other hand, the client is less comfortable or not quite ready to use floor markers, you can keep it simple with the use of post-it notes on their desk.

The essence of this exercise is to give the client an opportunity to sense-check a variety of options. These options could relate to potential career moves but could equally relate to discerning what options to offer to a new internal or external customer. The positioning can be adapted depending on where the individual is on their career journey.

This process enables another level of intelligence to surface. It can provide insights and information that might be just outside the conscious awareness of the client. Through this increased awareness, they are set up to further explore each of the options as required, before making a leap.

It also gives them a chance to check what they feel attracted to and what their energy is moving towards. This is vital information that can often be suppressed or ignored until it's too late. This is especially relevant if the client has been loyal to following a planned future that is potentially no longer relevant or serving them.

You can do this as often as is needed and it might make sense to check this a few times over the course of the coaching journey.

There are two options for this exercise:

Working 'blind'

You have the option of taking away the rational part of the brain completely by working 'blind'. This involves mapping the options in a way that the client doesn't know which option is which.

They are simply invited to check each and take a 'reading' of their energy and attraction factor. This approach can help the client get out of their own way and is especially helpful if they are too 'in their head' and have the tendency to close down their alternative intelligences.

Working transparently

In this scenario, the client chooses markers (paper or post-it notes) to represent each option and the options are written explicitly and remain visible throughout the exercise.

Step 1

Agree on the axes that will be most helpful. For example, if the client was reviewing options for their next role, the axes might be:

- Optimum for me and my family
- Optimum for my longer-term career

Step 2

Invite the client to take a few minutes to capture all of the options they are aware of and to create a marker (A4 paper or post-it note) for each one. I would also recommend creating an extra marker to represent the option that might come soon but is not yet on their radar – we'll call this option, 'something else'.

If you have decided to work blind with the client, simply ask them to put letters or numbers on each piece of paper. Behind the scenes, and out of sight of the client, decide which option pertains to which letter/number but don't tell them at this stage.

Step 3

When the axes are set out on the floor or on the desktop if you are working virtually, invite the client to place each marker (one at a time) wherever they feel compelled to do so, on the 2 x 2 matrix. This doesn't need to take loads of time. Ask them, and keep reminding them to trust their gut instinct rather than be driven by where they feel they should be placing each.

Step 4

When all markers are placed (blind or transparently) invite them to take a sense-check of the whole 'map' and check what they notice energetically and visually. They may feel immediately compelled to move something or indeed, move quite a few of the markers!

If they are working blind, then that is OK. If they are working transparently, however, this could just be a signal that the map in front of them doesn't match their internalised map of their planned future and in this scenario, it is suggested that they don't move anything yet.

Step 5

After harvesting that first reaction, invite them to spend a few moments checking out each option. If they have set this up on the floor, invite them to stand on each, and if it's on the desktop via post-it notes, just ask them to physically touch each one individually or hold each one in their 'mind's eye'.

With each option, represented by the marker, ask them how they are and what they notice. What is happening with their energy? To what degree do they sense the marker is in the right place relative to the axes? If this is the first time they have experienced the systemic approach, give them time to quieten down any internal noise that might create interference.

Remind them of their multiple intelligences and that this process will activate and help them receive important information from their heart and their gut. This is vital intelligence that might not have an opportunity to be surfaced otherwise.

After sensing into each, it is OK if they want to move the marker for a more accurate placing of where it belongs on each continuum.

When they have spent time on all markers, invite them once again to step back and look at the whole and check if they want to make any final adjustments to the placement of each.

If you have been working 'blind', you can now reveal what each marker represents in terms of options. Give the client time to take this in and to match what you've disclosed (the identity of each) with what they have experienced, how they felt about each, their energy throughout and in the present moment as they listen.

Step 6

Ensure the client has some reflection time to fully digest all of this data. Encourage them not to make any big decisions exclusively on this sensing. This process serves to surface more information about each option that might otherwise have been out of their awareness.

Invite them to let this intelligence emerge and with some time and space, it often makes complete sense. It will also significantly inform any further exploration required on the options reviewed.

This approach can also be very powerfully applied to a product or whole-business dimension. You would utilise the same mapping process as mentioned above and adjust the axes.

The way you label the axes has to be relevant for the client and their context. If you were working with a client who wanted to review their portfolio in terms of what is fit for the future, some suggestions for the two axes could be:

- What customers want from us
- Optimum value for our business/brand

I have utilised this approach on many occasions for my own business and particularly when I could sense that something needed to change but couldn't quite put my finger on the specifics.

As part of my own exploration of the upcoming future and gathering more understanding of what was calling me, I also utilised this mapping exercise. Public speaking and sharing the power of this approach came up as one of those areas that was of high value in the market whilst also enabling me to fully utilise my experience. It was within this exploration that the context of this book emerged.

Client example:

"I know I'm ready for something else, but I have no idea what it is, and it feels a bit daunting."

Hazel was a highly-respected specialist in the finance function of a global business. She had joined the company in the very early part of her career and had almost become 'part of the furniture'. She had dedicated herself to the job and to the business. Everyone knew her and loved her down-to-earth accessibility. She could talk to the receptionist and the CEO with equal levels of ease and authenticity.

Her brand was that of a consistent, loyal and trusted partner who delivered on brief, every time. She had moved through the organisation over her 20 plus years of service and had garnered huge credibility.

She had already landed her 'dream job' a few years previously and still had a lot left to give. However, her heart and soul were yearning for something else – something was missing and she couldn't quite put her 'finger on it'. The overriding brief for the coaching journey was to help her figure out what was next.

Through the coaching journey she discovered her calling. After much exploring, soul searching and connecting with the evolutionary force of her future, as described in the mapping process above, she realised that her destiny was no longer in corporate life.

She was being pulled to contribute to a different set of beneficiaries – the wider community. In particular, she was being called to dedicate her energy and expertise to help, nurture and develop young and under-privileged adults to enter the corporate world. It was her unique way of balancing out what she felt she had received in abundance over the course of her own career.

Equipped with this insight and clarity, she was able to navigate the subsequent six months to prioritise the completion of her priority projects, ensure her successor was ready, and gracefully exit the business with the send-off she deserved.

Some coaching assignments will result in the individual finding a new path and potentially leaving their current organisation. The reality is that the departure would most likely have happened anyway, but with a carefully-held coaching process, the exit can be proactively managed to secure a win: a win for both parties.

CHAPTER ELEVEN

STRENGTHEN THE SENSE OF PURPOSE

There is a lot of coverage on the theme of purpose – it is a hot topic that most people in business buy in to, at least in principle. My experience, however, is that in reality, they may not have necessarily found a meaningful and authentic way to distil this for themselves, without it feeling like another item on the should-do list.

In 2020, we experienced a decade's worth of change in one year! It is difficult to navigate this degree of change successfully without a sense of purpose. This context has provided an opportunity for a healthy reset on almost every dimension of life and work.

Recent research shared at The European Economic Forum in 2020 underscored the importance of purpose and its place at the heart of business. Over 60% of C-suite executives believe they need to have more responsible business practices. What businesses do versus what they say they will do is under more scrutiny than ever before. Employees are more discerning about how organisations do business – people can do incredible things when they know and understand what it's all for. Customers will follow companies that they trust with their money.

The top 3% of global businesses in the private sector review their success on both financial and societal measures. Whilst most companies have contracted during the global crisis of 2020/2021, this 3% of companies have expanded. If you need a business case to put emphasis on clarifying and leading with purpose, then this is it.

We are no longer a dictator society – we have shifted to become a movement society – people are looking to join a cause where they can emotionally engage with an organisation.

From a systemic perspective, a sense of purpose provides orientation, focuses the energy within the system and for the functions, teams and individuals within it. When employees have a sense of the organisational purpose, they can find their place relative to this purpose and also understand how they can contribute to it.

A recent example of how central purpose is, was very evident in the retail sector which was hit particularly hard by the disruption and crisis of the pandemic of 2019–2021. This pandemic stretched across the globe and during 2020 it reached crisis point in the UK, when the government felt that it had no option other than to force the majority of retail stores to shut their doors for the best part of 12 months. This period became known as 'lockdown'.

The value of a clear purpose was so evident within one of the major chains of department stores in the UK, the John Lewis Partnership. This retail giant was founded in 1864 and is the largest UK employee-owned business, with 78,000 employees who co-own the business via trust. Because of this unique ownership model, employees are called 'partners'.

Just before and throughout this period of 'lockdown', John Lewis was undertaking a strategic review within which they chose to start this process by going back into their history archives and reminding themselves of the founding purpose and principles of the organisation.

They spent time talking to all 'partners' and encouraged the sharing of stories from their history, eliciting special memories that dated back to their humble beginnings.

One of the key questions they posed was 'why are you proud to work here?' and went on to survey their suppliers and customers. Through this strategic process, everyone across the organisation was enlivened, empowered and energised by the reminder of their core purpose.

This provided a solid platform to reignite and focus the energy and resolve to serve UK citizens through the grocery arm of the business, Waitrose.

They redeployed people who were not able to work in the department stores into the grocery chains to ensure the shelves were replenished overnight for the frenzied rush by customers who sensed an urgent need to stock up supplies at home in case they were locked down at home for an extended period. What an inspiration!

Purpose creates meaning, orientation and galvanises energy in a system. It is a critical component of a healthy system and particularly key for providing an anchor point during times of significant change. It is important to regularly sense-check the evolution of the purpose as it can shift over time as the needs of society, customers and the upcoming future also evolve.

The process of uncovering purpose

From a systemic perspective, there are a number of ways in which you can approach the uncovering of purpose. These range from a semi-structured approach that incorporates some of the classic strategic planning dimensions through to more of a sensing approach, which is often called phenomenological, i.e. a non-structured approach that is more about working in the moment, trusting your multiple intelligences and working with what emerges.

Developing purpose with a group

When working with a group, it is helpful to create a living, 3D map of the organisation so that the discovery process moves from a predominately thought-based discussion to one that also incorporates a highly visual and visceral experience.

A 'living map' involves creating 'markers' for each of the key components of the ecosystem. It's recommended to do this using a large open space and place the markers on the floor, so that the participants can walk around and step into the ecosystem later in the process.

If you are working with a leadership team, for example, the ecosystem would include all of the internal functions, customers, partners in the supply chain, competitors, some elements of the wider ecosystem, e.g. local government and importantly, a 'marker' for the organisational purpose.

Even if they haven't done any work on purpose thus far, get them to create a 'marker' for purpose anyway – they will instinctively know the essence and direction of it and can embrace these principles as they place the marker for their purpose on the map. This process will, in fact, enable the articulation to emerge.

These markers can be as simple as pieces of A4 paper or to increase the power of the map, you can also use objects. My preference is the latter and I tend to use cardboard boxes of various sizes, ensuring each box is clearly identified as representing a specific element of the system.

One essential ingredient for each marker is the addition of an arrow, i.e. in addition to adding the name e.g. purpose, you are also adding an arrow so that when placed, the group can decide which direction the purpose is facing in the system.

Add arrows to all of the markers as this will also provide insight on who/what is facing what in the ecosystem as the map unfolds.

Create the as is perspective

Having identified and created all the relevant markers, ask the group to create their map of the ecosystem, by placing each of their markers in the space, based on their felt sense of how all the parts relate to each other currently. It's vital to emphasise that this phase is about mapping the current reality and *not* how they think it should be.

Make the most of the diverse perspectives in the group so that they can avoid the trap of trying to create the perfect map. Invite them to constructively challenge each other until they believe they have an accurate 'as is' picture.

Assuming you are working face to face, invite them to step into the ecosystem, or if you are working virtually via post-it notes or a virtual whiteboard, invite them to quieten down and connect with it intuitively.

Encourage them to trust what they notice about the energy, vitality and shape of the system. Ensure that all members of the team have a chance to step into the system and when you believe everyone has had the chance to take in the 'as is' picture, they are ready for some gentle provocation.

Here are some example questions you can offer:

- How much energy, vitality and potential for movement is here?

- What do our customers/consumers want from us?

- In context of the wider ecosystem, what might they need in the future?

- If we could make some adjustments to meet those needs, what would need to move?

As these questions resonate with the group, give them the opportunity to shift the markers as they see fit. Don't be surprised if there is a sudden rush to move quite a few of the markers. The important thing here is to give the group space and time to experiment.

When they believe they have moved what needs to be moved, give them some time to make sense of the new 'map' – create the opportunity for them to transfer this to some practical application.

A few recommended questions to offer at this stage of the process:

- What is this telling you?

- What needs attention?

- What needed to be adjusted?

- What still needs some adjustment?

- As you look at this, what is your sense of purpose and is it fit for the future?

- How can you engage your people in this?

Client example:

One of the world's biggest and most successful publishers was taking the opportunity to review the shape of the business in the context of a significantly shifting landscape. They are a privately-owned business where 60% of the portfolio was originally established by several generations of the family and the remaining component had been acquired from one of its biggest competitors.

The part of the business that was acquired had been through a series of transformations and changes in ownership – changing from a public limited company to private equity and then being split into parts before being sold off. It is fair to say that this part of the organisation (and the employees within it) had been through some challenging experiences, and absorbed in uncertainty about their future, over the course of a decade.

The combined organisation had huge brands, commanded the market share in the categories it published within and was well known for its efficiency. Employees were deeply loyal to their brands and believed they really knew their readers.

However, despite its size and commanding market share, it found itself challenged. There were revolutionary changes in consumer habits, including an accelerated shift towards digital. Whilst it had converted a few of the major brands to multiple platforms, this was not the case across the majority of the portfolio.

In fact, some of their biggest brands were declining and significantly lagging behind their competitors. A lot of attention was absorbed internally, including keeping tight control of the existing cost base. Much less attention was dedicated to figuring out how to adjust the ship or indeed change into another vessel to ride the waves of a turbulent and transforming marketplace.

A new CEO was appointed and then along came the pandemic! These volcanic-like eruptions, like most natural disasters, often galvanise the leadership team to stand together. This was the case in this organisation.

This eruption brought the leadership team together with an intention to look for a solution beyond the immediate crisis.

They zoomed out and from this perspective, mapped the wider system based on the 'as is' position. This included all of the parts of the business (functions and brands) as well as the owners, the consumers and the customers.

There were quite a few iterations of this map and when it settled, there was a strong visceral response to the realisation that the organisation was almost totally focused on the internal workings and especially facing the owners.

This 'as is' map provided a stark reality reminder of the fact that there was limited attention on consumers despite the seismic changes that were happening in the sector and in consumer habits.

Significant 'light bulb moments' later, they were invited to remap the system for the journey ahead. From this new map, they were able to articulate a purpose and a revised internal setup that would enable the business to reconnect with the consumer revolution and regain its momentum.

This provided clarity on how they needed to reshape the business at a functional level and also informed the optimum shape of the executive team. This new map created a solid platform for further conversations which were more appropriate at an individual level.

There was some fine-tuning required of this setup, but in a relatively short space of time, this leadership team had redefined their future trajectory, and anchored it in a purpose that refocused the business.

The systemic mapping of the system significantly informed how they needed to reshape the business, the functions and the teams in a way that fully engaged everyone in the co-creation process.

The individual dimension

From an individual perspective, purpose is critical. It acts as an anchor, an orienting force and provides an inner compass. Purposeless leaders create rudderless organisations.

Addressing individual purpose (before helping them with defining their organisational purpose) is paramount within the leadership coaching process.

The mapping exercise described within the client example above can also be utilised at an individual level.

You can also offer a less structured and less complex, but equally powerful, approach which involves inviting the individual to view their purpose in the context of a timeline, as per the outline below.

Step 1 – Create the elements

Ask the individual to create a few markers for each element of the ecosystem (with arrows) which they will set up on a timeline. There are just six markers required, as follows:

- **Current purpose** – that which is being lived – even if that has not been articulated up to this point.

- **Current customers** – ie those who they serve currently dependent on their role – this could be customers, society or internal colleagues.

- **New purpose** – the version that enables them to serve at the highest level.

- **New customers** – those who they will serve in the future.

- **Their upcoming future** – that which is calling them forwards, what life wants from them and will ultimately enable them to move towards their highest potential.

- **A marker for themselves ('ME')** – this will be helpful if they wish to place themselves on the timeline and then stand back and observe the whole picture with themselves in it.

Step 2 – Clarify orientation of the timeline

When all the markers have been created, invite the individual to identify an orientation towards the current time horizon and where the future is for them.

Step 3 – Create the 'as is' map

Ask them to place the markers pertaining to the current time horizon (current purpose and current customers) on the timeline so that they can gather some insights on the 'as is' situation.

Invite them to get a visceral sense of what's happening in relation to these two elements by stepping onto each marker.

As they view the map, encourage them to pay attention to a few key factors:

- How close or far away are the markers from each other?

- Who/what is facing who/what e.g. is the purpose facing the customers or facing elsewhere?

- Who is turning towards versus turning away?

- If they have created a marker for themselves – what/who is it facing?

Support them in their sensing by asking them to share what they notice. At this point, they may decide the markers need to be moved – allow this to happen as long as they are creating a more accurate sense of what is and not how they think it should be.

Step 4 – Acknowledge what is

Give them a moment to make sense of the 'as is' and through the conversation, amplify any dissatisfaction by drawing these insights to the surface – this is a healthy way to disrupt the current pattern and create some appetite and impetus for movement.

From a systemic perspective, we regard frustration as an expression of life energy that is simply blocked. This is better than low or no energy in the system.

Step 5 – Create the new map

Invite them to place the remaining markers (new customers, new purpose and upcoming future). When these have settled into their place on the timeline, invite the client onto these markers, one at a time.

Finish off this piece by inviting them to stand in the place of new customers and from there, view the new purpose through these lenses.

The role of the coach throughout is to help the individual harvest what they see, sense and feel, and bring these insights to the surface of their awareness so that they can process it fully, later.

Some helpful questions and provocations to offer:

- What's different about your current customers and your new customers – is there a relationship between these?

- What do you sense new customers need from you?

- What do you notice about your position relative to your purpose?

- What comes to mind/what is happening with your energy when you stand on your new purpose?

- When you stand on your new purpose, what (in your mind's eye) are you looking at?

- In what direction is your energy pulled?

It's important not to rush this process – there is a lot of data and intelligence being gathered beyond the rational thinking brain. Create a sense of spaciousness.

In this work we often use the phrase: "The body knows and the head will catch up."

Step 6 – Creating space for reflection sense-making

When the client has had enough time harvesting their visceral experience, provide some space for them to start the sense-making process. Replaying what they noticed and what they said as the process unfolded is incredibly helpful at this stage.

They may need some reflection time before being able to articulate the new purpose and if so, ensure to finish this session by capturing some themes for them to take away.

Client Example

Releasing the limiting pattern creates space for the next phase of growth.

We met Archie, a high performer with a solid track record in the previous chapters. There was no question about his expertise and experience. He had over a decade of specialist experience under his belt but the perceptions of his leadership brand were getting in the way.

He was perceived by his key stakeholders as leading from a place of ego and charm. In an organisation where the narrative matters, this was creating an unnecessary limitation on his career potential.

The feedback was that he needed to do some work on his leadership brand as he was seen as needing to be in the spotlight and operating from a strong ego. His peers felt he was too close to his line manager, in his partnering relationship, to the extent that they did not feel he could be a vital and neutral sounding board or provide objective thought leadership.

When we leverage the systemic approach, we dig deeper beyond the behavioural dimension. We get to the source of the repeating, limiting pattern and ensure this is fully acknowledged and included in the client's history.

In addition to mapping Archie's organisational history, we unpacked his personal system. He was the youngest of two boys and always felt like his older brother was in the spotlight within the family and by comparison, he felt like he was in the shadows.

He found a way to operate in this family system by overachieving, by playing full out as a strategy to get the attention he craved.

This unconsciously held pattern was also showing up in his leadership. As this was a genuine blind spot for him, he had not realised where this came from but once we got to the root cause in his personal system, he was able to fully acknowledge and include the insights from this difficult experience.

This process of honouring all of his history and acknowledging what is, including the limiting patterns and where they came from, set him up for the next step.

Having acknowledged the root cause which set him up to have the relevant conversations in his family, he was able to be released from this unconscious pattern. He was able to get the attention he craved in his family, in a more conscious and considered way.

Once released, he no longer had to be in the centre of things within the organisational context − he could let this unconscious compensatory strategy fall away and create the space for something new.

The next step was to help him start to engage with his upcoming future and help him craft a sense of purpose which was about setting others up for success and partnering with the business in the context of his senior leadership role.

He reviewed his values and fine-tuned these in alignment with his new purpose, and then set about embedding this into his everyday behaviour.

Within a relatively short period of time, he had dramatically transformed his leadership brand. A fantastic example of this was at their annual company conference, where he shifted from being perceived to be in the limelight and 'master of ceremonies' the year before, to providing the stage for his team (who had done all the hard work).

He ensured he was 'at their back' and supported as a sounding board in the background. More importantly, in this new context, he also felt much more fulfilled.

Fast-forward 24 months, and Archie has secured that top global role in his field of expertise. His leadership brand as an enabler and developer of talent has been consolidated.

Summary

The topic of purpose is very current but also critically important from a leadership perspective. Purposeless leaders create rudderless organisations. This is a critical step in the HARNESS coaching process.

The systemic approach enables the purpose to emerge and evolve within the context of the wider ecosystem.

PERCOLATIONS...

As a coach who constantly operates in service of others, it's easy to neglect our own sense of purpose and how this is evolving.

Take some time to review this:

- What is your sense of purpose?

- Is this still valid?

- Does it still energise you?

- Would your clients resonate with this?

- Take note of what kind of work/what kind of clients are coming towards you. This can also be a signal – what are the patterns?

- Are you connecting to your upcoming future, and if so, what is being asked of you?

- Anything need to be adjusted?

....

FIND YOUR VOICE

I can't hear you – it's too loud, it's too crowded in this
conversation…

It's all about you and yet,

I know you are putting yourself into the world in the only way
you know how

So why don't I show up? Where is my voice?

I can't hear myself speak – the stories in my head are too loud

The many reasons why I perceive you won't hear me, see me,
or even acknowledge me

So why don't I show up – where's my voice?

And yet to be authentic

There doesn't need to be any stories – in me, or in me, about you

You are being you – and I can still be me

With clarity, strength, space and calm

I need to discover

What's here for me? What's true for me?
What sits right within me?

And then, there is

MY VOICE.

....

CHAPTER TWELVE

SOLIDIFY LEADERSHIP BRAND

What do we mean by leadership brand?

When I use the phrase 'brand' in the context of leadership, what do I mean?

It is a phrase more often used for products and in this context, we are talking about the core values and attributes you automatically associate with that brand.

For example, if we consider Primark, one of the large and growing global retail chains, some of the things that come to mind include mass market, low cost, low- or medium-quality fashion and quite contemporary in style. Primark is probably also seen as providing clothing that is of the high street and of the moment. In short, its brand positioning is probably well summarised as contemporary and inexpensive.

On the other hand, if we were to consider another global clothing brand such as Gucci, a very different set of attributes are likely to come to mind, including exclusive, quality and expensive. These brands have very different core values that enable each product to find their unique place in the fashion industry.

We have similar examples in other industries. In the food industry, Asda, which is part of Walmart has a clear brand, best known for 'everyday low prices' whereas in the tech industry, Apple is best known for constant innovation, quality and beautiful designs that break industry norms.

In the context of leaders who have the responsibility for others, the concept of brand is very similar, and becoming more important.

As we know from research, the attributes and style of leadership impacts the climate in an organisation (what it feels like to work there) by up to 70%. What you stand for, what you stand against (your core values) and your dominant behaviours are becoming more important than ever.

Employees are becoming vigilant of, and sensitive about, the core values and moral compass of organisations and their leaders. Wider societal issues such as reducing your carbon footprint for the sake of the planet and eradicating modern slavery in the global supply chain are things that matter.

As mentioned before, we are no longer a dictator society, we are becoming more and more of a movement society. Developing or transforming a clear and consistent leadership brand is an important part of the development of a leader in the current context.

On a very simple level, when we think about leadership brand, a very helpful question to keep in mind is what would people say about you or how would they describe you, if you weren't here?

It's important, however, to dig deeper, especially if you want to enable a sustainable step change in behaviours. You need to get to the drivers and root cause of those behaviours. We need to expose the deeper layers demonstrated within the visual below and this is where the systemic approach can add significant value.

If people were to sum you up, in just a few words – what would they be?

What behaviours can we expect from you?

What unique value do you bring?

What do you stand for? What do you stand against? (core values)

Why are you here? (purpose)

Who are you? (identity)

As human beings, we can pick up incongruence quickly. When you can stand congruently and operate consistently in each of the layers highlighted in the visual overleaf, people will know what they are getting when they engage with you. This predictability provides an unconscious level of safety and you will be perceived as trustworthy.

Within the coaching journey, this final element of the 'Harness' framework is about bringing all the pieces together for consolidation. The earlier components are needed first, in order for the leadership brand work to be meaningful, believable and sustainable.

The 360 feedback gathered in the 'Acknowledge Current Reality' phase will have provided valuable insight into how someone is showing up at the start of the coaching process and how they are currently perceived. This will have provided clarity on their current leadership brand and ignited deep reflections on the degree to which change is required.

The behaviours identified will have been informed, to some degree, by the individual's history – both personal and organisational. Whilst honouring and respecting this history, you will have uncovered and hopefully identified and released some of the limiting patterns, thereby freeing them up to create a new sense of identity and brand.

By enabling them to get a sense of what the evolutionary force of the upcoming future is asking of them, you will have created some urge and potency for forward movement. By contrast, clarifying their sense of purpose will have provided a level of being more grounded and will have helped them to feel appropriately anchored.

Bringing it all together

Now it's time to bring it all together through solidifying their leadership brand.

In the first instance, the aim is to help the individual have a level of internal clarity, certainty and cohesion so that they can subsequently articulate to others who they are and what people can expect from them.

Of course, the essential ingredient for an authentic brand is to also consistently deliver on this declaration.

The questions you are helping the client to articulate for themselves are detailed within the visual below:

1. Who are you? (your sense of identity.)

2. Why are you here? (purpose.)

3. What do you stand for and what do you stand against? (core values.)

4. What value do you add? (your unique contribution/impact on the business, people and society.)

5. What kind of behaviours can we expect to see from you?

6. If people were to sum you up in just a few words, how would you want people to describe you?

Encouraging the individual to do some preparation themselves before this final stage of the process is incredibly helpful and important.

I'd recommend asking them to reflect on each of the steps in the coaching process so far. It can be helpful to provide them with some themes and questions to support their thinking.

Suggested preparation brief

- Review the history mapping and your journey thus far as a leader – who are you and how has this been informed by your history?

- Whose shoulders do you stand upon?

- Review your 360 feedback that was initiated at the start of the process – what elements do you want to ensure you carry forward?

- What patterns have served you that you will consciously bring with you?

- Which patterns have now reached their expiry date?

- How would you want your stakeholders to be describing you, moving forwards? (shifting from ? to ?)

- What is important to you? What do you want to stand for as a leader? Of equal importance, what do you stand against/ not stand for?

- What is your purpose – why are you here? And how will you know your contribution has been of value?

- What is calling you forward? What is the upcoming future asking from you? How can you leverage your unique offering for the benefit of others?

Having devoted sufficient reflection time to all of the above (and reviewed their notes from the various sessions thus far) this final stage of the coaching process is about solidifying, fine-tuning and integrating.

This session (or series of sessions) can be undertaken face to face or virtually. If you are working face to face, it is recommended that you fully utilise the space in the room to create a visual and visceral experience for and with the individual.

If you are working virtually, you can support the individual to do this within their space as you observe them, or another alternative is to invite them to use post-it notes on the desktop.

The following outline is based on a face-to-face session but can be very easily adjusted, for the virtual environment.

The overall map

Step 1 – Ingredients for the map

Ask the individual to create 'markers' (with arrows) for the following elements:

- Their history (this can be denoted by a marker for *each* of the organisations they have been part of, up to this point OR if they have been in one organisation for a long time, then each of the key roles they have had in that organisation.)

- Their 'old' sense of identity (how people described them in their initial 360 feedback report.)

- The patterns they are leaving behind.

- Their core values – maximum of five (what is important to them.)

- Their capabilities (skills, knowledge and experience.)

- The patterns they want to *bring with them.*

- Their refreshed purpose.

Step 2 – Identify the timeline

Invite the individual to create a timeline in the space, clarifying which end of the room denotes history, where the present time horizon is in the space and which end of the room denotes the future.

Step 3 – Create the map

Ask them to map out each of the markers above on the timeline. It is important not to rush this part of the process. Just by adding these to the prescribed timeline, a significant process is going on within the individual.

At an unconscious level, we are introducing healthy endings by asking them to identify and acknowledge the parts of themselves that will always be incorporated within their history but no longer need to be carried forwards. This 'healthy endings' process, when handled well, can create space for new beginnings.

Step 4 – Gathering resources

When all markers have been placed, invite them to firstly sense-check with themselves if anything needs to be adjusted. Encourage them to trust their instinct and intuition rather than relying totally on logic or rational thinking.

When any fine-tuning has settled, invite them to step into the space that is denoted as the present time.

If their core values are not already near them, it might be helpful to adjust these, so that they are close enough to feel like a resource.

Invite them to notice their capabilities – and check the optimum location for these. Once again, having them relatively close by will be resourcing and strengthening for them.

Check where the marker for their purpose is – ensure it's in their line of sight and if it isn't, ask them what is needed in order for this to be on their horizon. Allow any adjusting that is needed for this to happen.

Give them time to settle in this position. Encourage them to notice how this feels here and what they sense. Invite them to 'lock this in' as an internal picture so it can 'drop into' muscle memory and be available for recall, when they are being temporarily blown off course.

Step 5 – Look back before moving forwards

This acknowledgement step is a vitally important step in the process of moving forwards. Invite them to turn around and face the various markers relating to their history (organisations, job roles, old identity and old patterns).

Offer them the following sentences to say out loud or internally as they acknowledge this history:

"You are and will always be part of my history. Without you, I would not be who I am today. I am grateful for all these experiences and those who have contributed to them – I have learned a lot."

It is not unusual, however, to find that there can be some resistance to this acknowledgement phase, and especially if the individual has had some tough experiences up to this point. If this is the case, offer them a precursor to the same sentences: *"I hate to admit it, but…"*

Step 6 – Distil the leadership brand

When the acknowledgement has settled and seems sincere, get them to turn around again – still standing on the present timeline and facing their upcoming future.

Invite them to stand on their purpose and engage with their future, with their core values, capabilities and enabling patterns close by as resources.

This is rich territory – expect to harvest quite a lot of information in terms of what they are noticing, how they are feeling and any movements or adjustments they want to make. It is not unusual for them to move their resources around.

If they seem a bit shaky/inconsistent, experiment with moving their resources (healthy patterns, core values and capabilities) until such time as they seem more solid and robust in their sense of who they are.

Once they have settled here, this is the opportunity to distil and clarify the leadership brand that they are moving towards.

Here are some questions to support this part of the process:

1. Who are you here (identity)?

2. What are you here to do (purpose)?

3. What's important to you (values)?

4. What do you stand for (values)?

5. What do you stand against (core values)?

6. What can people expect from you (behaviours)?

7. If people were to sum this version of you up in just a few words, what words would they use?

Capture and harvest their responses to each of the above, so you can give them the notes later for the final reflection and refinement process.

You are now ready to decide with the individual when would be an optimum time to initiate the next iteration of 360 feedback. I would recommend creating a few months of space between this final phase and gathering feedback – this will give the individual time to integrate this work and build momentum in this new way of showing up in their system.

Client example

We met Derek, the CFO who was moved to a new divisional role, in previous chapters.

His stakeholder feedback suggested that he was more than qualified for the role. There were, however, a few areas to work on in terms of his sense of place, in that he was seen and experienced as being a bit on the periphery rather than part of the team. This was having an impact on the flow of leadership at the executive team level.

The CEO & CFO relationship is really significant in most businesses and this was also the case in this organisation. However, Derek's CEO was making a really clear request for a trusted business partner and confidant relationship – something that had not yet been established in the first six months of their working relationship.

Over the course of a 12-month coaching journey, Derek reviewed his history map. This created the platform to more accurately pinpoint the root cause of this discomfort in the 'number two' seat.

Space and time were dedicated to figuring out his sense of place in the team and in the business, as well as pinpointing where his resistance to settling into the team was coming from.

We worked through a combination of distortions and disruptions in his personal system as well as the organisational context. Having done the 'deeper work' to understand and subsequently release these limiting patterns, we took time to distil, and make concrete, the new behaviours that Derek could authentically step into.

Finally, Derek uncovered a purpose that not only served him, but it also served his CEO and the wider system. He undertook a thorough review of his core values and created an internal code of conduct for himself. Twelve months later, feedback from his key stakeholders, which included his CEO, suggested that he has become a vital and fully integrated member of the team. His wisdom and counsel are sought by all.

From a performance perspective, this new level of integration and camaraderie within the executive team has enabled Derek to engage his peers to drive a seven-figure saving across the division. This achievement and return on investment were too outrageous to even consider at the outset of this coaching assignment!

Summary

The concept of leadership brand sounds more complex than it needs to be. By now you will have helped your client work through all of the component parts.

This phase is about bringing it all together and doing a final sense-check – how do they want to show up in the system now that they are free of their limiting patterns, clearer on their purpose and engaged with what the world wants from them.

FINAL PERCOLATIONS...

As the coach, and potentially a leader in your own right, take some time to explore your own landscape and answer these questions for yourself:

1. Who are you? (identity.)

2. What are you here to do? (purpose.)

3. What's important to you and why? (core values.)

4. What do you stand for? (core values.)

5. What do you stand against? (core values.)

6. What can people expect from you? (behaviours.)

7. If people were to sum this version of you up in just a few words, what words would they use?

A few words to close....

The systemic approach is about facilitating two key movements for and with your clients/colleagues:

1. Release any limiting patterns that might be hindering flow, freedom or performance – bear in mind, these will be operating unconsciously.

2. Create a sense of clarity of the upcoming future so that individuals, groups or organisations can move towards their highest potential.

For the client, it provides a whole person perspective and encourages an openness to dig deep. When taken seriously, the shift is sustainable and the rewards are worth it.

For the coach, this is an invitation to uplevel your approach. The pandemic of 2019/2021 has fused the worlds of work, home and life. It is time to work with the whole person.

We need to build our skills such that we can handle the messy and the complex. This approach requires spaciousness. We need to feel comfortable in the not knowing, to go back and to go deep in order to create forward momentum. It is about knowing when to go deep and when to cut through the noise.

Now is the time to invest in your coaching toolkit.

HARNESS is intended to provide food for thought, healthy provocation, examples of real-world application and a range of practical tools for immediate impact.

I'd love to hear your reflections on HARNESS and if you'd like more information on the systemic coaching approach, please do get in touch.

tess@thetransformationagency.com

Endnotes

1   Research from Monster, reporting strong signals of burnout in those working extensively from home: Dealing with burnout when working from home | Mind, the mental health charity – help for mental health problems

2   The Triple Bottom Line: What It Is & Why It's Important (hbs.edu)

3   Can the legacy of trauma be passed down the generations? – BBC Future

4   How the heart and brain are communicating with each other : https://www.heartmath.org/research/science-of-the-heart/heart-brain-communication/

About the Author

Tess is an ICF accredited leadership coach with over 25 years' experience in cultural transformation and leadership development across a wide range of sectors.

She has held a variety of commercial positions in preparation for her step through to senior HR roles, which have included board level responsibility. She is actively working with leaders, and leadership teams across the UK, Europe, Asia Pac, Middle East and the US.

Tess lives in the UK with her family and a menagerie of pets, which include her herd of three horses. On occasion, these three geldings have been known to bring immense value to the coaching process!

www.thetransformationagency.com